Introduction

This book offers a cooperative, engaging approach to meet and exceed the middle school and high school Language Arts Standards set forth by the National Council for Teachers of English and the International Reading Association. The standards establish expectations for students and teachers. However, teachers have wide latitude for how they teach to reach academic goals. Many English/language arts teachers rely on traditional instructional strategies. The teacher lectures or leads the class in discussions. While a direct instruction model has a place in every language classroom, it is not the only mode of instruction, nor always the best.

Language arts standards call for comprehension, interpretation, and evaluation of texts. The standards encourage speaking skills and effective communication. And they ask that students participate as knowledgeable, reflective, creative, and critical members of a variety of literacy communities. Cooperative instructional strategies provide students the opportunities to interact, discuss, tutor, and practice their communication skills in a way not possible without student-to-student interaction. Breaking the class into smaller groups and into pairs gives each student more opportunities to participate. Instead of being in one large class, the student is now one in a small group or even one in a pair. In the teacher-led classroom, there is only one or two active participants in the class at a time—the teacher and a student. In the cooperative learning classroom, there is at least one student in every pair or team that is actively engaged. When we look at how much more engaged students are in cooperative groups, it is no wonder they learn more, keep on task more, and enjoy learning more.

In addition to the quantity of interactions, look too at the quality of interactions in the cooperative classroom. Student-to-student interactions can be used to deepen students' understanding of texts and language arts content. Explaining a concept or discussing a book makes the content more meaningful and memorable. Interactions empower students to become active learners, rather than passive recipients of information. To learn something well, students must be engaged and active, asking questions and discussing their learning. Students learn best by doing. The activities in this book are based on Kagan Cooperative

Learning Structures—simple promote student interaction across the language curriculum. The structures create student discussion, cooperation, quizzing, peer tutoring, and communication—all effective processes for mastering the language arts content. The structures are designed to engage every student in learning. Each student plays an active role with each structure, thereby increasing the probability of success for even reluctant learners. Students who might not fully participate in a whole-class setting are now highly encouraged to participate on an ongoing basis. The structure of the task requires everyone to keep tuned in and stay on task.

Most students enjoy the opportunities to interact with peers and find cooperative learning more motivating. Some structures are whole-class interactions; others are completed in small groups or in pairs. These structures provide review, self-assessment, class discussion, and skill development.

Book Organization

Six Kagan Cooperative Learning Structures are presented throughout this book. Step-by-step instructions and tips are provided to make it easy to learn and use the structure in your classroom. The structures were selected because they are particularly good for teaching and learning language arts content. For example, Quiz-Quiz-Trade is a fun and engaging way for students to review need-to-know language arts curriculum. Teammates Consult provides the opportunity for students to practice communication skills and share information and knowledge.

Cooperative Learning Structures boost active engagement. More active learning enhances motivation and promotes language arts content mastery and skill development.

Following each structure are a number of activities and resource pages to use with the structure. The content provided is a sampling of language arts curriculum and skills for grades 7–12. The ready-to-use activities allow you to try the various structures. We hope you will try the sample activities provided and witness firsthand the powerful impact the structures have on student motivation and learning. There are also a number of blackline templates for you to create your own materials to use with the structures. It is our hope that not only will you use the ready-to-use activities provided, but also learn the structures well and integrate these active learning strategies frequently into your daily teaching.

Acknowledgments

The materials for this book are a compilation of Structure lessons based on Language Arts Standards for grades 7–12. A project such as this cannot be completed without the assistance of others.

This book has grown through years of teaching experiences and ideas shared through conversations with colleagues and teammates. Other ideas have been developed through attendance at educational workshops and conferences.

A thank-you to my friend and former colleague, Alisa Krehbiel, for testing some of the activities and providing valuable feedback.

This book would not have come to fruition without the encouragement and guidance of Dr. Jacqueline Minor, Director of School Improvement Programs for Kagan Professional Development. Her assistance, insights, and constructive feedback have given me confidence in completing this work.

Appreciation goes to Miguel Kagan, Director of Publications for believing in me and reviewing the manuscript. Thanks to his team of designers: Alex Core for book design and production; Heather Malk contributing designer; Becky Herrington, Publications Manager; Erin Kant, Illustrator; and Kim Fields, Copy Editor.

Table Of Contents

Structure 1
Fan-N-Pick............**9**

Structure 2
Inside-Outside-Circle...........................**35**

Structure 3
Quiz-Quiz-Trade...............................**71**

Structure 4
RallyCoach 170

Structure 6
Teammates Consult 207

Structure 5
RoundRobin 195

Chart of Language Arts Elements

	Pages	Characters	Text Types	Novel Elements	Vocabulary
Fan-N-Pick					
Cause and Effect	12–16		★		
Vocabulary	17–21				★
Confusing Homophones	22–27				★
Idioms	28–32				★
Inside-Outside Circle					
Vocabulary Whirlwind	38–40				★
The Grapes of Wrath— Novel Vocabulary Review	41–45				★
Quotes & Statements Discussion Cards	46–52	★		·	★
Borrowed Words	53–57				·
*The Adventures of Tom Sawyer—*Novel Review	58	·		★	
*The Pearl—*Novel Review	59–63	·		★	
Idioms	64–68				★
Quiz-Quiz-Trade					
Literary Terms	74–80	★		★	★
*Julius Caesar—*Character Cards	81–85	★		★	
A Tale of Two Cities— Character Cards	86–89	★		★	
Confused Words	90–94				★
Latin Root Word Meanings and Examples	95–100				★
Latin Prefixes and Suffixes	101–106				★
Greek Root Word Meanings	107–111				★
Greek Prefixes and Suffixes	112–116				★
Elements of a Short Story	117–120			★	
Text Types—Definitions	121–125		★		
Text Types—Structures	126–130		★		
Text Types—Examples	131–135		★		
Text Types—Structures with Graphic Organizers	136–145		★		
Figurative Language Definitions	146–150				★
Figurative Language Examples	151–160				★
Homophones	161–167				★

Chart of Language Arts Elements *(continued)*

	Pages	Characters	Text Types	Novel Elements	Vocabulary
RallyCoach					
Idioms and Meanings	172–177				★
Suffixes	180				★
Romeo and Juliet—Themes	181	★		★	
The Pearl—Symbolism	182–183	★		★	
The Pearl—Characterization/Master	184–186	★		·	
Parts of Speech Worksheet 1 & 2	187–188				★
Vocabulary Words	190				★
RoundRobin (Cubes)					
Cause and Effect Cube	198		★		
Compare and Contrast Cube	199		★		
Problem and Solution Cube	200		★		
Description Cube	201		★	★	
Sequence Cube	202		★		
Reading Cube	203	★		★	
Story Cube	204	★		★	
Teammates Consult					
Of Mice and Men—Character Sketch	210	★		★	
Any Novel—Character Sketch	211	★		★	
A Tale of Two Cities—Discussion Prompts	212	★		★	
Night—Timeline of Important Events	213			★	
Idioms and Idiom Recoding Sheet	214–219				★
Building Characterization	220	★		★	
To Build a Fire—Writing About a Novel	221	★		★	

English Standards for Language Arts
National Council for Teachers of English
International Reading Association

1. Students read a wide range of print and non-print texts to build an understanding of texts, of themselves, and of the cultures of the United States and the world; to acquire new information; to respond to the needs and demands of society and the workplace; and for personal fulfillment. Among these texts are fiction and nonfiction, and classic and contemporary works.

2. Students read a wide range of literature from many periods in many genres to build an understanding of the many dimensions (e.g., philosophical, ethical, aesthetic) of human experience.

3. Students apply a wide range of strategies to comprehend, interpret, evaluate, and appreciate texts. They draw on their prior experience, their interactions with other readers and writers, their knowledge of word meaning and of other texts, their word identification strategies, and their understanding of textual features (e.g., sound-letter correspondence, sentence structure, context, graphics).

4. Students adjust their use of spoken, written, and visual language (e.g., conventions, style, vocabulary) to communicate effectively with a variety of audiences and for different purposes.

5. Students employ a wide range of strategies as they write and use different writing process elements appropriately to communicate with different audiences for a variety of purposes.

6. Students apply knowledge of language structure, language conventions (e.g., spelling, punctuation), media techniques, figurative language, and genre to create, critique, and discuss print and non-print texts.

7. Students conduct research on issues and interests by generating ideas and questions, and by posing problems. They gather, evaluate, and synthesize data from a variety of sources (e.g., print and non-print texts, artifacts, people) to communicate their discoveries in ways that suit their purpose and audience.

8. Students use a variety of technological and informational resources (e.g., libraries, databases, computer networks, video) to gather and synthesize information and to create and communicate knowledge.

9. Students develop an understanding of and respect for diversity in language use, patterns, and dialects across cultures, ethnic groups, geographic regions, and social roles.

10. Students whose first language is not English make use of their first language to develop competency in the English language arts and to develop understanding of content across the curriculum.

11. Students participate as knowledgeable, reflective, creative, and critical members of a variety of literacy communities.

12. Students use spoken, written, and visual language to accomplish their own purposes (e.g., learning, enjoyment, persuasion, the exchange of information).

Fan-N-Pick

Structure I

Fan-N-Pick

Teammates play a card game to respond to questions.
Roles rotate with each new question.

Group Size
Teams of Four

Steps

Setup: Each team receives a set of question cards.

1 **Student #1 Fans Cards**
Student #1 holds the question cards in a fan (concealing the answer side) and says, *"Pick a card, any card!"*

2 **Student #2 Picks a Card**
Student #2 picks a card, reads the question aloud, and allows five seconds of think time.

3 **Student #3 Answers**
Student #3 answers the question.

4 **Student #4 Responds**
Student #4 responds to the answer:
- For right or wrong answers, Student #4 checks and then either praises or tutors.
- For questions that have no right or wrong answer, Student #4 does not check for correctness, but praises and then paraphrases the thinking that went into the answer.

5 **Rotate Roles**
Students rotate roles, one person clockwise for each new round.

Tips
- Laminate cards for future use.
- Show students how to fan cards so they do not reveal the answer.

Activities

Blank Fan-N-Pick Cards Template...33

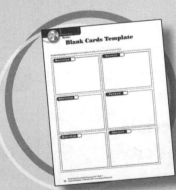

Blank Fan-N-Pick Cards Template...34

Cause and Effect

Directions: Copy one set of cards per team. Cut out each card along the dotted line. Fold each card along the solid line so you have the question on one side and the answer on the other. Cards may be glued or taped to keep questions and answers on opposite sides. Students should keep answer section hidden.

Question **1**	**Answer** **1**
People cut down trees to clear land for new homes. Cutting down the trees destroys the animal habitats. *Cause and Effect*	**Cause:** People cut down trees to clear land for new homes. **Effect:** Cutting down the trees destroys the animal habitats. *Cause and Effect*
Question **2**	**Answer** **2**
Large ponds are drained. The wildlife is decreasing. *Cause and Effect*	**Cause:** Large ponds are drained. **Effect:** The wildlife is decreasing. *Cause and Effect*
Question **3**	**Answer** **3**
Radioactive materials are leaking into the city's drinking water. An earthquake occurred near the power plant. *Cause and Effect*	**Cause:** An earthquake occurred near the power plant. **Effect:** Radioactive materials are leaking into the city's drinking water. *Cause and Effect*

Cause and Effect (continued)

Directions: Copy one set of cards per team. Cut out each card along the dotted line. Fold each card along the solid line so you have the question on one side and the answer on the other. Cards may be glued or taped to keep questions and answers on opposite sides. Students should keep answer section hidden.

Question 4

Turning off electronic equipment and lights when leaving the house is a way to save energy.

Saving energy is an important way to help the environment.

Cause and Effect

Answer 4

Cause: Turning off electronic equipment and lights when leaving the house is a way to save energy.

Effect: Saving energy is an important way to help the environment.

Cause and Effect

Question 5

A balanced diet is part of a healthy lifestyle.

Eating well can result in a longer and healthier life.

Cause and Effect

Answer 5

Cause: A balanced diet is part of a healthy lifestyle.

Effect: Eating well can result in a longer and healthier life.

Cause and Effect

Question 6

Farmers need to buy more land so they can raise larger crops.

The decrease in the market price of corn is hurting the farmers.

Cause and Effect

Answer 6

Cause: The decrease in the market price of corn is hurting the farmers.

Effect: Farmers need to buy more land so they can raise larger crops.

Cause and Effect

Cause and Effect (continued)

Directions: Copy one set of cards per team. Cut out each card along the dotted line. Fold each card along the solid line so you have the question on one side and the answer on the other. Cards may be glued or taped to keep questions and answers on opposite sides. Students should keep answer section hidden.

Question 7

Many Southerners must cut back on water to conserve the little they have left.

The Southern United States has suffered months of serious drought.

Cause and Effect

Answer 7

Cause: The Southern United States has suffered months of serious drought.

Effect: Many Southerners must cut back on water to conserve the little they have left.

Cause and Effect

Question 8

Torrential rains drenched the campsite and soaked sleeping bags.

The campers staked their tents even though cloudy weather lingered overhead.

Cause and Effect

Answer 8

Cause: The campers staked their tents even though cloudy weather lingered overhead.

Effect: Torrential rains drenched the campsite and soaked sleeping bags.

Cause and Effect

Question 9

Sports enthusiasts supported their winning team throughout the season.

With continued support, the Falcons rallied to win the championship.

Cause and Effect

Answer 9

Cause: Sports enthusiasts supported their winning team throughout the season.

Effect: With continued support, the Falcons rallied to win the championship.

Cause and Effect

Cause and Effect (continued)

Directions: Copy one set of cards per team. Cut out each card along the dotted line. Fold each card along the solid line so you have the question on one side and the answer on the other. Cards may be glued or taped to keep questions and answers on opposite sides. Students should keep answer section hidden.

Question 10

Airports posted delayed and cancelled flights that were making departures difficult for holiday travelers.

Blizzard and icing conditions created havoc along the eastern coast.

Cause and Effect

Answer 10

Cause: Blizzard and icing conditions created havoc along the eastern coast.

Effect: Airports posted delayed and cancelled flights that were making departures difficult for holiday travelers.

Cause and Effect

Question 11

Exercise is a good way to build a healthy body.

Many people who exercise have healthy hearts.

Cause and Effect

Answer 11

Cause: Exercise is a good way to build a healthy body.

Effect: Many people who exercise have healthy hearts.

Cause and Effect

Question 12

When the oceans become polluted, the coral reefs die.

Dumping waste into our oceans creates changes in the environment.

Cause and Effect

Answer 12

Cause: Dumping waste into our oceans creates changes in the environment.

Effect: When the oceans become polluted, the coral reefs die.

Cause and Effect

Cause and Effect *(continued)*

Directions: Copy one set of cards per team. Cut out each card along the dotted line. Fold each card along the solid line so you have the question on one side and the answer on the other. Cards may be glued or taped to keep questions and answers on opposite sides. Students should keep answer section hidden.

Question 13

The gentleman was confined to his wheelchair.

His arthritis was a debilitating disease.

Cause and Effect

Answer 13

Cause: His arthritis was a debilitating disease.

Effect: The gentleman was confined to his wheelchair.

Cause and Effect

Question 14

Some of Frank's favorite subjects were history and politics.

Frank taught history at his alma mater for twenty years.

Cause and Effect

Answer 14

Cause: Some of Frank's favorite subjects were history and politics.

Effect: Frank taught history at his alma mater for twenty years.

Cause and Effect

Question 15

The basketball team earned their fourth consecutive league title.

Coach Royson trained his team to demonstrate leadership, teamwork, and respect for all.

Cause and Effect

Answer 15

Cause: Coach Royson trained his team to demonstrate leadership, teamwork, and respect for all.

Effect: The basketball team earned their fourth consecutive league title.

Cause and Effect

Vocabulary

Directions: Copy one set of cards per team. Cut out each card along the dotted line. Fold each card along the solid line so you have the question on one side and the answer on the other. Cards may be glued or taped to keep questions and answers on opposite sides. Students should keep answer section hidden.

Question 1	Answer 1
Define the underlined word. The price of gasoline was rising at a <u>disarming</u> rate. *Vocabulary*	**Disarming:** alarming *Vocabulary*

Question 2	Answer 2
Define the underlined word. I'll ignore the <u>frivolous</u> comment regarding the evening's performance. *Vocabulary*	**Frivolous:** not worthy of serious attention *Vocabulary*

Question 3	Answer 3
Define the underlined word. The Boston Red Sox attracted <u>fervent</u> fans during their entire season. *Vocabulary*	**Fervent:** passionate *Vocabulary*

Question 4	Answer 4
Define the underlined word. It is wise to have a lawyer <u>peruse</u> your document before you sign it. *Vocabulary*	**Peruse:** read thoroughly and carefully *Vocabulary*

Question 5	Answer 5
Define the underlined word. As a result of the devastating tornado, the victims looked rather <u>haggard</u>. *Vocabulary*	**Haggard:** fatigued *Vocabulary*

Question 6	Answer 6
Define the underlined word. A <u>residue</u> of tar spattering left the vehicle difficult to clean. *Vocabulary*	**Residue:** remainder *Vocabulary*

Vocabulary (continued)

Directions: Copy one set of cards per team. Cut out each card along the dotted line. Fold each card along the solid line so you have the question on one side and the answer on the other. Cards may be glued or taped to keep questions and answers on opposite sides. Students should keep answer section hidden.

Question 7 Define the underlined word. The friends made a plan to <u>rendezvous</u> at the team center after the game. *Vocabulary*	**Answer 7** **Rendezvous:** a meeting location *Vocabulary*
Question 8 Define the underlined word. The bicycling club members tended to attract those who were of a <u>kindred</u> spirit and appreciated the beauty of nature and new challenges. *Vocabulary*	**Answer 8** **Kindred:** being of a similar nature or character *Vocabulary*
Question 9 Define the underlined word. The night sky was picturesque and as <u>mesmerizing</u> as a host of glittering objects. *Vocabulary*	**Answer 9** **Mesmerizing:** fascinating *Vocabulary*
Question 10 Define the underlined word. Looking back he realized that if he had a <u>modicum</u> of sense, he would have made better preparations for his rock-climbing trip. *Vocabulary*	**Answer 10** **Modicum:** small portion or limited quantity *Vocabulary*
Question 11 Define the underlined word. The Internet provides information on a <u>myriad</u> of topics. *Vocabulary*	**Answer 11** **Myriad:** great number *Vocabulary*
Question 12 Define the underlined word. My mother was absolutely <u>livid</u> that I had failed my entrance exam. *Vocabulary*	**Answer 12** **Livid:** very angry *Vocabulary*

Vocabulary (continued)

Directions: Copy one set of cards per team. Cut out each card along the dotted line. Fold each card along the solid line so you have the question on one side and the answer on the other. Cards may be glued or taped to keep questions and answers on opposite sides. Students should keep answer section hidden.

Question 13

Define the underlined word.

<u>Scavengers</u> rummaged through the bins behind the row of restaurants.

Vocabulary

Answer 13

Scavengers: persons who collect or salvage garbage or junk

Vocabulary

Question 14

Define the underlined word.

His reputation as a <u>meticulous</u> individual served as an asset to the interview team.

Vocabulary

Answer 14

Meticulous: extreme or excessive care given to details

Vocabulary

Question 15

Define the underlined word.

The airline's sudden overhaul of equipment caused the public to <u>speculate</u> about the industry's problem.

Vocabulary

Answer 15

Speculate: to think or theorize about something

Vocabulary

Question 16

Define the underlined word.

During Henry's time at the convention, he visited with a <u>pleiad</u> of entrepreneurs who were there to share their knowledge.

Vocabulary

Answer 16

Pleiad: a group of seven outstanding people or things

Vocabulary

Question 17

Define the underlined word.

Her musical performance ranged from a <u>repertoire</u> of opera to classical selections.

Vocabulary

Answer 17

Repertoire: range of supplies or skills possessed by a person

Vocabulary

Question 18

Define the underlined word.

The brilliant colors of the <u>nebula</u> could be observed through the telescope in their backyard.

Vocabulary

Answer 18

Nebula: cloud of dust and gas in outer space

Vocabulary

Vocabulary (continued)

Directions: Copy one set of cards per team. Cut out each card along the dotted line. Fold each card along the solid line so you have the question on one side and the answer on the other. Cards may be glued or taped to keep questions and answers on opposite sides. Students should keep answer section hidden.

Question 19

Define the underlined word.

Maggie's high level of diplomacy and professionalism impressed her underlined{colleagues}.

Vocabulary

Answer 19

Colleagues: persons or associates with whom one works in an office or profession

Vocabulary

Question 20

Define the underlined word.

The holiday underlined{luminaries} served as guiding lights to each of the homes along the avenue.

Vocabulary

Answer 20

Luminaries: something that gives light

Vocabulary

Question 21

Define the underlined word.

The plans for the graduation party came to underlined{fruition} sooner than they expected.

Vocabulary

Answer 21

Fruition: enjoyment of a desired outcome when it happens

Vocabulary

Question 22

Define the underlined word.

As the younger brother, Jeff practiced diligently to underlined{emulate} his brother's talent on the basketball court.

Vocabulary

Answer 22

Emulate: to imitate or strive to excel

Vocabulary

Question 23

Define the underlined word.

As a underlined{vivacious} hostess, she had the ability to make her guests comfortable as they mingled during the party.

Vocabulary

Answer 23

Vivacious: lively or spirited

Vocabulary

Question 24

Define the underlined word.

The noise at the back door and the sound of glass breaking underlined{raddled} guests during the middle of the night.

Vocabulary

Answer 24

Raddled: a state of confusion or lacking composure

Vocabulary

Vocabulary *(continued)*

Directions: Copy one set of cards per team. Cut out each card along the dotted line. Fold each card along the solid line so you have the question on one side and the answer on the other. Cards may be glued or taped to keep questions and answers on opposite sides. Students should keep answer section hidden.

Question 25

Define the underlined word.

As the runners struggled with the weather elements, it became clear this was a test of each runner's <u>fortitude</u>.

Vocabulary

Answer 25

Fortitude: the strength of mind and courage to deal with situations during adversity

Vocabulary

Question 26

Define the underlined word.

At the conclusion of the service, the organist played the <u>postlude</u> while the worshipers stood in silence.

Vocabulary

Answer 26

Postlude: a closing piece of music at the end of a service, especially a church service

Vocabulary

Question 27

Define the underlined word.

The student was not willing to <u>jeopardize</u> his grade by skipping classes.

Vocabulary

Answer 27

Jeopardize: to expose to danger or risk

Vocabulary

Question 28

Define the underlined word.

The builder had a reputation for using only the most <u>durable</u> products when constructing homes.

Vocabulary

Answer 28

Durable: able to exist for a long time without major deterioration

Vocabulary

Question 29

Define the underlined word.

The <u>ramshackle</u> house on the edge of town had been an eyesore for many years.

Vocabulary

Answer 29

Ramshackle: something that is old, in poor shape, ready to collapse

Vocabulary

Question 30

Define the underlined word.

The levy served as a <u>buttress</u> for the city as the waters continued to rise.

Vocabulary

Answer 30

Buttress: something that supports, gives stability, or strengthens

Vocabulary

Confusing Homophones

Directions: Copy one set of cards per team. Cut out each card along the dotted line. Fold each card along the solid line so you have the question on one side and the answer on the other. Cards may be glued or taped to keep questions and answers on opposite sides. Students should keep answer section hidden.

Question 1

What is the difference between these homophones?

1. Gait

2. Gate

Confusing Homophones

Answer 1

1. Gait: a walking pace
2. Gate: the entrance to a fenced area

Confusing Homophones

Question 2

What is the difference between these homophones?

1. Feat

2. Feet

Confusing Homophones

Answer 2

1. Feat: an achievement requiring strength and courage
2. Feet: plural of foot, which is a lower extremity of the leg

Confusing Homophones

Question 3

What is the difference between these homophones?

1. Oar

2. Ore

Confusing Homophones

Answer 3

1. Oar: a pole with a flat blade for steering through water
2. Ore: a solid material from which a metal mineral can be profitably extracted

Confusing Homophones

Question 4

What is the difference between these homophones?

1. Coarse

2. Course

Confusing Homophones

Answer 4

1. Coarse: rough or loose in texture or grain
2. Course: a route or direction often followed by a ship, aircraft, road, or river

Confusing Homophones

Question 5

What is the difference between these homophones?

1. Faze

2. Phase

Confusing Homophones

Answer 5

1. Faze: to disturb
2. Phase: a period of time

Confusing Homophones

Question 6

What is the difference between these homophones?

1. Council

2. Counsel

Confusing Homophones

Answer 6

1. Council: a group that meets to plan and inform
2. Counsel: giving professional help and advice to someone

Confusing Homophones

Confusing Homophones (continued)

Directions: Copy one set of cards per team. Cut out each card along the dotted line. Fold each card along the solid line so you have the question on one side and the answer on the other. Cards may be glued or taped to keep questions and answers on opposite sides. Students should keep answer section hidden.

Question 7
What is the difference between these homophones?
1. Peak
2. Peek
3. Pique
Confusing Homophones

Answer 7
1. *Peak:* the pointed top of a mountain
2. *Peek:* to look at quickly
3. *Pique:* to stimulate one's interest in something
Confusing Homophones

Question 8
What is the difference between these homophones?
1. Hardy
2. Hearty
Confusing Homophones

Answer 8
1. *Hardy:* tough, being able to withstand difficult situations
2. *Hearty:* vigorous and cheerful
Confusing Homophones

Question 9
What is the difference between these homophones?
1. Bazaar
2. Bizarre
Confusing Homophones

Answer 9
1. *Bazaar:* a market or fund raising sale with different types of goods
2. *Bizarre:* strange or unusual
Confusing Homophones

Question 10
What is the difference between these homophones?
1. Board
2. Bored
Confusing Homophones

Answer 10
1. *Board:* a flat piece of wood
2. *Bored:* a lack of interest
Confusing Homophones

Question 11
What is the difference between these homophones?
1. Die
2. Dye
Confusing Homophones

Answer 11
1. *Die:* to stop living
2. *Dye:* to add a natural or synthetic substance that will cause a change in color
Confusing Homophones

Question 12
What is the difference between these homophones?
1. Weather
2. Whether
Confusing Homophones

Answer 12
1. *Weather:* refers to the state of atmospheric conditions
2. *Whether:* a choice between alternatives
Confusing Homophones

Confusing Homophones (continued)

Directions: Copy one set of cards per team. Cut out each card along the dotted line. Fold each card along the solid line so you have the question on one side and the answer on the other. Cards may be glued or taped to keep questions and answers on opposite sides. Students should keep answer section hidden.

Question 13

What is the difference between these homophones?

1. Pour

2. Pore

Confusing Homophones

Answer 13

1. Pour: to flow from some type of container
2. Pore: a very small opening in the surface

Confusing Homophones

Question 14

What is the difference between these homophones?

1. Forth

2. Fourth

Confusing Homophones

Answer 14

1. Forth: moving forward from a starting point, out into the open
2. Fourth: the number four in sequence

Confusing Homophones

Question 15

What is the difference between these homophones?

1. Capital

2. Capitol

Confusing Homophones

Answer 15

1. Capital: an important city or the seat of government in a place
2. Capitol: the building housing a legislative assembly

Confusing Homophones

Question 16

What is the difference between these homophones?

1. Which

2. Witch

Confusing Homophones

Answer 16

1. Which: to ask for information about a specific set of things
2. Witch: a woman thought to have evil powers

Confusing Homophones

Question 17

What is the difference between these homophones?

1. Principle

2. Principal

Confusing Homophones

Answer 17

1. Principle: a truth serving as part of one's belief system
2. Principal: a person with high authority in an organization or institution

Confusing Homophones

Question 18

What is the difference between these homophones?

1. Stationary

2. Stationery

Confusing Homophones

Answer 18

1. Stationary: not moving
2. Stationery: writing paper, usually with matching envelopes

Confusing Homophones

Confusing Homophones (continued)

Directions: Copy one set of cards per team. Cut out each card along the dotted line. Fold each card along the solid line so you have the question on one side and the answer on the other. Cards may be glued or taped to keep questions and answers on opposite sides. Students should keep answer section hidden.

Question 19

What is the difference
between these homophones?

1. Allude

2. Elude

Confusing Homophones

Answer 19

1. Allude: to hint at something indirectly
2. Elude: to evade or escape
from danger or something

Confusing Homophones

Question 20

What is the difference
between these homophones?

1. Brake

2. Break

Confusing Homophones

Answer 20

1. Brake: a device used to
slow or stop a moving vehicle
2. Break: to separate into pieces

Confusing Homophones

Question 21

What is the difference
between these homophones?

1. Pedal

2. Petal

3. Peddle

Confusing Homophones

Answer 21

1. Pedal: a foot-operated
lever used to control a vehicle
2. Petal: the segments of a flower
3. Peddle: trying to sell something
by going from house to house

Confusing Homophones

Question 22

What is the difference
between these homophones?

1. Ceiling

2. Sealing

Confusing Homophones

Answer 22

1. Ceiling: the top surface
of a room or a container
2. Sealing: a device or substance
used to lock two things together

Confusing Homophones

Question 23

What is the difference
between these homophones?

1. Stair

2. Stare

Confusing Homophones

Answer 23

1. Stair: a set of steps leading
from one floor of a building to another
2. Stare: a fixed or vacant look
at someone or something for a period
of time, usually with one's eyes wide open

Confusing Homophones

Question 24

What is the difference
between these homophones?

1. Haul

2. Hall

Confusing Homophones

Answer 24

1. Haul: to pull or drag with
effort or to transport with a vehicle
2. Hall: an area in a building
that leads to other rooms

Confusing Homophones

Confusing Homophones (continued)

Directions: Copy one set of cards per team. Cut out each card along the dotted line. Fold each card along the solid line so you have the question on one side and the answer on the other. Cards may be glued or taped to keep questions and answers on opposite sides. Students should keep answer section hidden.

Question 25

What is the difference between these homophones?

1. Beach

2. Beech

Confusing Homophones

Answer 25

1. Beach: a pebbly or sandy shore at a lake or ocean
2. Beech: a large tree that produces fruit: the beechnut

Confusing Homophones

Question 26

What is the difference between these homophones?

1. Suite

2. Sweet

Confusing Homophones

Answer 26

1. Suite: a set of rooms designated for a particular purpose
2. Sweet: having a pleasant taste of sugar or honey

Confusing Homophones

Question 27

What is the difference between these homophones?

1. Sheer

2. Shear

Confusing Homophones

Answer 27

1. Sheer: to swerve or change course quickly; or a very thin piece of fabric
2. Shear: to cut the wool off as on sheep; or a break in a structure caused by some type of strain

Confusing Homophones

Question 28

What is the difference between these homophones?

1. Feinted

2. Fainted

Confusing Homophones

Answer 28

1. Feinted: a pretend blow or mock attack meant to distract someone as in boxing or in warfare
2. Fainted: weak or dizzy; appearing feeble or lacking strength

Confusing Homophones

Question 29

What is the difference between these homophones?

1. Warn

2. Worn

Confusing Homophones

Answer 29

1. Warn: to inform someone in advance of pending danger or a potential problem
2. Worn: damaged and shabby as a result of use; the past tense of wear

Confusing Homophones

Question 30

What is the difference between these homophones?

1. Steal

2. Steel

Confusing Homophones

Answer 30

1. Steal: to take without permission
2. Steel: iron used as a building material

Confusing Homophones

Confusing Homophones *(continued)*

Directions: Copy one set of cards per team. Cut out each card along the dotted line. Fold each card along the solid line so you have the question on one side and the answer on the other. Cards may be glued or taped to keep questions and answers on opposite sides. Students should keep answer section hidden.

Question 31 What is the difference between these homophones? *1. Right* *2. Write* *Confusing Homophones*	**Answer 31** *1. Right:* something that is true, correct, or acceptable *2. Write:* using letters, words, or symbols to record or communicate information on a surface such as paper *Confusing Homophones*
Question 32 What is the difference between these homophones? *1. Dough* *2. Doe* *Confusing Homophones*	**Answer 32** *1. Dough:* a soft mixture of flour and liquid used in baking bread or pastry *2. Doe:* a female deer *Confusing Homophones*
Question 33 *Confusing Homophones*	**Answer 33** *Confusing Homophones*
Question 34 *Confusing Homophones*	**Answer 34** *Confusing Homophones*
Question 35 *Confusing Homophones*	**Answer 35** *Confusing Homophones*
Question 36 *Confusing Homophones*	**Answer 36** *Confusing Homophones*

Idioms

Directions: Copy one set of cards per team. Cut out each card along the dotted line. Fold each card along the solid line so you have the question on one side and the answer on the other. Cards may be glued or taped to keep questions and answers on opposite sides. Students should keep answer section hidden.

Question 1

Explain the meaning of the idiom.

ace up your sleeve

Idioms

Answer 1

Having a special advantage that is not used until the very last moment.

Idioms

Question 2

Explain the meaning of the idiom.

barking up the wrong tree

Idioms

Answer 2

You are giving your attention or focus to the wrong thing.

Idioms

Question 3

Explain the meaning of the idiom.

all ears

Idioms

Answer 3

Being ready to listen carefully.

Idioms

Question 4

Explain the meaning of the idiom.

bury the hatchet

Idioms

Answer 4

To settle an argument or put the past behind you.

Idioms

Question 5

Explain the meaning of the idiom.

I'm at the end of my rope.

Idioms

Answer 5

Not being able to take it any more, being tired of the situation.

Idioms

Question 6

Explain the meaning of the idiom.

crying wolf

Idioms

Answer 6

To give a false alarm. To say there is something happening when it's not.

Idioms

Idioms (continued)

Directions: Copy one set of cards per team. Cut out each card along the dotted line. Fold each card along the solid line so you have the question on one side and the answer on the other. Cards may be glued or taped to keep questions and answers on opposite sides. Students should keep answer section hidden.

Question 7	**Answer 7**
Explain the meaning of the idiom. **eating out of your hand** *Idioms*	To have control of someone or of a group of people. *Idioms*
Question 8	**Answer 8**
Explain the meaning of the idiom. **fair-weather friend** *Idioms*	Someone who is a friend only when things are good. *Idioms*
Question 9	**Answer 9**
Explain the meaning of the idiom. **off the hook** *Idioms*	To get out of doing something unpleasant. *Idioms*
Question 10	**Answer 10**
Explain the meaning of the idiom. **go fly a kite** *Idioms*	To tell someone to go away and stop bothering you. *Idioms*
Question 11	**Answer 11**
Explain the meaning of the idiom. **drop me a line** *Idioms*	To send me a letter or an e-mail. *Idioms*
Question 12	**Answer 12**
Explain the meaning of the idiom. **Let's call it a day.** *Idioms*	To say we should be finished for today. *Idioms*

Idioms (continued)

Directions: Copy one set of cards per team. Cut out each card along the dotted line. Fold each card along the solid line so you have the question on one side and the answer on the other. Cards may be glued or taped to keep questions and answers on opposite sides. Students should keep answer section hidden.

Question 13

Explain the meaning of the idiom.

to get a kick out of something

Idioms

Answer 13

To find something amusing.

Idioms

Question 14

Explain the meaning of the idiom.

to get one's wires crossed

Idioms

Answer 14

To be confused or mistaken about something.

Idioms

Question 15

Explain the meaning of the idiom.

go with the flow

Idioms

Answer 15

To take things as they come.

Idioms

Question 16

Explain the meaning of the idiom.

to pull someone's leg

Idioms

Answer 16

To tease someone by trying to make him or her believe something that is exaggerated or untrue.

Idioms

Question 17

Explain the meaning of the idiom.

tight fisted

Idioms

Answer 17

Someone who is very frugal and unwilling to spend money unnecessarily.

Idioms

Question 18

Explain the meaning of the idiom.

to bite off more than one can chew

Idioms

Answer 18

To take on responsibility for more than one can manage.

Idioms

Idioms *(continued)*

Directions: Copy one set of cards per team. Cut out each card along the dotted line. Fold each card along the solid line so you have the question on one side and the answer on the other. Cards may be glued or taped to keep questions and answers on opposite sides. Students should keep answer section hidden.

Question 19 Explain the meaning of the idiom. **fender bender** *Idioms*	**Answer 19** A small automobile accident. *Idioms*
Question 20 Explain the meaning of the idiom. **let sleeping dogs lie** *Idioms*	**Answer 20** Don't cause problems by doing something when it isn't necessary. *Idioms*
Question 21 Explain the meaning of the idiom. **leave well enough alone** *Idioms*	**Answer 21** To do nothing because doing something would make the situation worse. *Idioms*
Question 22 Explain the meaning of the idiom. **make a mountain out of a molehill** *Idioms*	**Answer 22** To make something seem much more important than it really is. *Idioms*
Question 23 Explain the meaning of the idiom. **keep one's chin up** *Idioms*	**Answer 23** To remain brave and be confident in a difficult situation and not to worry too much about it. *Idioms*
Question 24 Explain the meaning of the idiom. **know something backward and forward** *Idioms*	**Answer 24** To know or understand something very well, thoroughly. *Idioms*

Idioms (continued)

Directions: Copy one set of cards per team. Cut out each card along the dotted line. Fold each card along the solid line so you have the question on one side and the answer on the other. Cards may be glued or taped to keep questions and answers on opposite sides. Students should keep answer section hidden.

Question 25 Explain the meaning of the idiom. **at the eleventh hour** *Idioms*	**Answer 25** **Waiting to do something until the very last minute when it is almost too late.** *Idioms*
Question 26 Explain the meaning of the idiom. **cost someone an arm and a leg** *Idioms*	**Answer 26** **The item may cost a lot or be very expensive.** *Idioms*
Question 27 Explain the meaning of the idiom. **keep one's nose to the grindstone** *Idioms*	**Answer 27** **To continue working so that one can complete his or her work on time.** *Idioms*
Question 28 Explain the meaning of the idiom. **quick study** *Idioms*	**Answer 28** **Someone who learns new things quickly and easily.** *Idioms*
Question 29 Explain the meaning of the idiom. **wear out one's welcome** *Idioms*	**Answer 29** **To make someone uncomfortable by visiting too long.** *Idioms*
Question 30 Explain the meaning of the idiom. **state of the art** *Idioms*	**Answer 30** **Using the latest technology.** *Idioms*

Blank Cards Template

Teacher Directions: Use this Blank Card template to make your own cards for Fan-N-Pick.

Question	Answer
Question	Answer
Question	Answer
Question	Answer
Question	Answer
Question	Answer

Blank Cards Template

Teacher Directions: Use this Blank Card template to make your own cards for Fan-N-Pick.

Question	Answer

Question	Answer

Question	Answer

Inside-Outside Circle
Structure 2

Structure 2

Inside-Outside Circle

Students rotate in concentric circles to face new partners for sharing, quizzing, or problem solving.

Group Size
Whole Class

Steps

Setup: The teacher prepares questions, or provides a question card for each student.

1 Form Outside Circle
Students form pairs. One student from each pair moves to form one large circle in the class facing outward.

2 Form Inside Circle
Remaining students find and face their partners (class now stands in two concentric circles).

3 Inside Circle Asks Question; Outside Circle Responds
Inside Circle students ask a question from their question card; Outside Circle students answer. Inside Circle students praise or coach.

4 Partners Switch Roles
Partners switch roles: Outside Circle students ask, listen, then praise or coach.

5 Partners Trade Cards
Partners trade question cards.

6 Rotate
Inside Circle students rotate clockwise to a new partner. (The teacher may call rotation numbers: "*Rotate Three Ahead.*" The class may do a "choral count" as they rotate.)

Teacher Questions:
Instead of giving each student a question card, the teacher can keep all the questions. The teacher asks the question, then indicates if the inside or outside circle student responds. For discussion questions, both partners can respond to the same question.

Variations:
Inside-Outside Line
Students stand in two straight lines facing each other. After each question, one line shifts, and the other remains in place so students face new partners. When the line shifts, the last student is not facing anyone. The last student walks to the other side of the line and pairs up with the first person in the fixed line.

Tips
- If you don't have enough cards for every student, it is ok to give the same card to multiple students.
- If you have more cards than students, you can give some students more than one card to use.
- When played with cards, steps 3–6 are Quiz-Quiz-Trade (see pages 74–168 for an example).
- Laminate cards for future use.

Activities

**Blank Inside-Outside Circle
Cards Template...69**

**Blank Inside-Outside Circle
Cards Template...70**

Vocabulary Whirlwind

Vocabulary Whirlwind Instructions

Vocabulary Whirlwind uses Inside-Outside Circle, Vocabulary Words, and Prompt Cards to teach vocabulary. The teacher prepares a list of vocabulary words associated with a short story or novel that students are reading. See *A Raisin in the Sun* examples on page 40. The teacher provides each student with one Prompt Card. The teacher reads a word from the vocabulary list. Students respond based on the Prompt Card they have.

Steps:

1 Each student receives a Prompt Card.

2 Students form two concentric circles. One is an inside circle, and the other is the outside circle.

3 The teacher announces which circle is Partner A and which circle is Partner B.

4 The teacher has a list of vocabulary words for review. See page 44 for a list of words and definitions from the novel, *A Raisin in the Sun*.

5 The teacher announces the vocabulary word (for example, *chauffeur*).

6 Partners A and B look at their Prompt Cards. (See Prompt Cards on page 39.) Partner A may have the card for **Parts of Speech** while Partner B may have the card for **Synonym**.

7 Partner A shares with Partner B the **Parts of Speech** for the given vocabulary word. "Chauffeur *is a common noun.*"

8 Then Partner B shares with Partner A the **Synonym** for the given vocabulary word. "*A synonym for* chauffeur *is driver.*"

9 The partners trade Prompt Cards and rotate to a new partner as the teacher gives rotation directions and announces a new vocabulary word.

10 If the partners cannot come up with an answer, they need to raise their hands and partner with a pair next to them.

Vocabulary Whirlwind
Prompt Cards

Directions: Use these Prompts Cards for all Vocabulary Whirlwind activities. Copy enough cards so each student receives a card. Cut out the cards along the dotted line.

Prompt Card

Definition

Vocabulary Whirlwind

Prompt Card

Sentence

Vocabulary Whirlwind

Prompt Card

Parts of Speech

Vocabulary Whirlwind

Prompt Card

Antonym

Vocabulary Whirlwind

Prompt Card

Add a Prefix or Suffix

Vocabulary Whirlwind

Prompt Card

Create a Simile

Vocabulary Whirlwind

Prompt Card

Synonym

Vocabulary Whirlwind

Prompt Card

Make a Rhyming Word

Vocabulary Whirlwind

Vocabulary Whirlwind Examples

Ⓐ *Raisin in the Sun*

Chauffeur: a person employed to drive a private or rented car

Elaborate: careful arrangement of parts or details

Exotic: originating in or characteristic of a distant foreign country

Refrain: to stop oneself from doing something; repeated lines or number of lines in a poem or song

Defiance: open resistance; bold disobedience

Contradictions: a combination of statements or ideas that are opposed to each other

Indictment: a formal charge or accusation of a serious crime

Vaguely: something of uncertain, indefinite, or unclear meaning

Mirage: an optical illusion caused by atmospheric conditions; something that appears real or possible but is not so

Penetrated: to succeed in forcing into or through something; to infiltrate or succeed in gaining insight into something

Falter: to start to lose strength or momentum; speaking in an unsteady voice or moving in an unsteady manner, showing a lack of confidence

Reverie: the state of being pleasantly lost in one's own thoughts like a daydream

Precariously: not in a secure position or about ready to fall; being dependent on chance; uncertain

Assimilation: to take in information and understand it

Incredulity: being unwilling or unable to believe something

Quizzical: puzzled amusement in one's expression or behavior

Profoundly: intense; severe

Acutely: difficult or unwelcome experience of an intense degree; having or showing a perceptive understanding or insight

Heritage: property that is or may be inherited

Vengeance: punishment inflicted or retribution exacted for an injury or wrongful deed

Recitation: to repeat aloud a poem or verse from memory before an audience

Insinuate: to suggest or hint at something in an indirect way

Enthusiasm: intense and excited enjoyment, interest, or approval

Vigorously: being strong, healthy, and full of energy

Neurotic: abnormally sensitive, obsessive, or tense and anxious

Sacrifice: surrendering an object as an offering to God or a supernatural figure

Oppressive: unjustly inflicting hardship on a group; something that weighs heavily on the mind, body, and spirit and causes distress

Diminish: to make or become less

Stereotype: a widely held, but fixed, image of a person or thing

Ominous: giving the impression that something bad is about to happen

The Grapes of Wrath
Novel Vocabulary Review

Directions: Copy the Vocabulary Review cards for *The Grapes of Wrath* by John Steinbeck, one per student. Cut out each card along the dotted line. Fold each card along solid line so the vocabulary word is on one side and the definition is on the other.

Vocabulary Word 1	Definition 1
Chambray	**Cotton material, plain color**
The Grapes of Wrath Vocabulary Review	*The Grapes of Wrath Vocabulary Review*

Vocabulary Word 2	Definition 2
Fetlocks	**Tufts of hair above the hoof of a horse**
The Grapes of Wrath Vocabulary Review	*The Grapes of Wrath Vocabulary Review*

Vocabulary Word 3	Definition 3
Petulant	**Rude language or speech**
The Grapes of Wrath Vocabulary Review	*The Grapes of Wrath Vocabulary Review*

Vocabulary Word 4	Definition 4
Incredulous	**Skeptical**
The Grapes of Wrath Vocabulary Review	*The Grapes of Wrath Vocabulary Review*

Vocabulary Word 5	Definition 5
Citadel	**A stronghold**
The Grapes of Wrath Vocabulary Review	*The Grapes of Wrath Vocabulary Review*

Vocabulary Word 6	Definition 6
Parapet	**A wall barrier**
The Grapes of Wrath Vocabulary Review	*The Grapes of Wrath Vocabulary Review*

The Grapes of Wrath
Novel Vocabulary Review (continued)

Directions: Copy the Vocabulary Review cards for *The Grapes of Wrath* by John Steinbeck, one per student. Cut out each card along the dotted line. Fold each card along solid line so the vocabulary word is on one side and the definition is on the other.

Vocabulary Word 7	Definition 7
Swale	**Low stretch of land**
The Grapes of Wrath *Vocabulary Review*	The Grapes of Wrath *Vocabulary Review*

Vocabulary Word 8	Definition 8
Bluster	**Sound off**
The Grapes of Wrath *Vocabulary Review*	The Grapes of Wrath *Vocabulary Review*

Vocabulary Word 9	Definition 9
Ravenous	**Hungry, eager for food**
The Grapes of Wrath *Vocabulary Review*	The Grapes of Wrath *Vocabulary Review*

Vocabulary Word 10	Definition 10
Benediction	**The giving of a blessing**
The Grapes of Wrath *Vocabulary Review*	The Grapes of Wrath *Vocabulary Review*

Vocabulary Word 11	Definition 11
Vigilante	**Taking the law into one's own hands**
The Grapes of Wrath *Vocabulary Review*	The Grapes of Wrath *Vocabulary Review*

Vocabulary Word 12	Definition 12
Ravine	**Long and deep hollow, gully, or canyon**
The Grapes of Wrath *Vocabulary Review*	The Grapes of Wrath *Vocabulary Review*

The Grapes of Wrath
Novel Vocabulary Review *(continued)*

Directions: Copy the Vocabulary Review cards for *The Grapes of Wrath* by John Steinbeck, one per student. Cut out each card along the dotted line. Fold each card along solid line so the vocabulary word is on one side and the definition is on the other.

Vocabulary Word 13	**Definition** 13
Stealthy	Being secretive or sneaky
The Grapes of Wrath Vocabulary Review	*The Grapes of Wrath Vocabulary Review*
Vocabulary Word 14	**Definition** 14
Cantankerous	Bad tempered
The Grapes of Wrath Vocabulary Review	*The Grapes of Wrath Vocabulary Review*
Vocabulary Word 15	**Definition** 15
Zenith	The highest point
The Grapes of Wrath Vocabulary Review	*The Grapes of Wrath Vocabulary Review*
Vocabulary Word 16	**Definition** 16
Drone	Monotonous
The Grapes of Wrath Vocabulary Review	*The Grapes of Wrath Vocabulary Review*
Vocabulary Word 17	**Definition** 17
Fatuous	Silly, foolish
The Grapes of Wrath Vocabulary Review	*The Grapes of Wrath Vocabulary Review*
Vocabulary Word 18	**Definition** 18
Tributary	Stream that leads to larger body of water
The Grapes of Wrath Vocabulary Review	*The Grapes of Wrath Vocabulary Review*

The Grapes of Wrath
Novel Vocabulary Review *(continued)*

Directions: Copy the Vocabulary Review cards for *The Grapes of Wrath* by John Steinbeck, one per student. Cut out each card along the dotted line. Fold each card along solid line so the vocabulary word is on one side and the definition is on the other.

Vocabulary Word 19	**Definition** 19
Caravan The Grapes of Wrath *Vocabulary Review*	**Group of vehicles traveling together** The Grapes of Wrath *Vocabulary Review*
Vocabulary Word 20	**Definition** 20
Prodigal The Grapes of Wrath *Vocabulary Review*	**Wasteful, extravagant** The Grapes of Wrath *Vocabulary Review*
Vocabulary Word 21	**Definition** 21
Shoat The Grapes of Wrath *Vocabulary Review*	**Young hog** The Grapes of Wrath *Vocabulary Review*
Vocabulary Word 22	**Definition** 22
Feral The Grapes of Wrath *Vocabulary Review*	**Wild, ferocious** The Grapes of Wrath *Vocabulary Review*
Vocabulary Word 23	**Definition** 23
Lithe The Grapes of Wrath *Vocabulary Review*	**Flexible** The Grapes of Wrath *Vocabulary Review*
Vocabulary Word 24	**Definition** 24
Eminent The Grapes of Wrath *Vocabulary Review*	**Distinguished, outstanding** The Grapes of Wrath *Vocabulary Review*

The Grapes of Wrath
Novel Vocabulary Review *(continued)*

Directions: Copy the Vocabulary Review cards for *The Grapes of Wrath* by John Steinbeck, one per student. Cut out each card along the dotted line. Fold each card along solid line so the vocabulary word is on one side and the definition is on the other.

Vocabulary Word 25	**Definition** 25
Inveterate	Habitual
The Grapes of Wrath Vocabulary Review	*The Grapes of Wrath Vocabulary Review*
Vocabulary Word 26	**Definition** 26
Truculent	Defiant or aggressive
The Grapes of Wrath Vocabulary Review	*The Grapes of Wrath Vocabulary Review*
Vocabulary Word 27	**Definition** 27
Cowl	Hood, head covering
The Grapes of Wrath Vocabulary Review	*The Grapes of Wrath Vocabulary Review*
Vocabulary Word 28	**Definition** 28
Rakish	Streamlined
The Grapes of Wrath Vocabulary Review	*The Grapes of Wrath Vocabulary Review*
Vocabulary Word 29	**Definition** 29
Venerate	With a high regard, revere
The Grapes of Wrath Vocabulary Review	*The Grapes of Wrath Vocabulary Review*
Vocabulary Word 30	**Definition** 30
The Grapes of Wrath Vocabulary Review	*The Grapes of Wrath Vocabulary Review*

Quotes & Statements
Discussion Cards

Directions: Copy so each student has a card. Cut out each card along the dotted line.

Student Card

"C'mon Joey. If you wanna see a rainbow, you gotta put up with a little rain."
—*"Dennis the Menace"* cartoon

Explain what this means to you.

Quotes & Statements

Student Card

"A perfect summer day is when the sun is shining, the breeze is blowing, the birds are singing, and the lawn mower is broken."
—*James Dent (1928–1992), American humorist and newspaper columnist*

Describe your "perfect" summer day.

Quotes & Statements

Student Card

"To the old, the new is usually bad news."
—*Eric Hoffer*

Do you think this is true? Why?

Quotes & Statements

Student Card

"Hindsight is foresight without a future."
—*Quote from movie, Music and Lyrics*

What are examples of this?

Quotes & Statements

Quotes & Statements
Discussion Cards (continued)

Directions: Copy so each student has a card. Cut out each card along the dotted line.

Student Card

"Rank does not confer privilege or give power. It imposes responsibility."
—*Peter Drucker*

What do you think this means?

Quotes & Statements

Student Card

What can our government do to help the homeless?

Quotes & Statements

Student Card

Do you think parents should use computer software to track their child's school records and behaviors? Is this responsible parenting?

Quotes & Statements

Student Card

What can students do to stop global warming?

Quotes & Statements

Quotes & Statements
Discussion Cards *(continued)*

Directions: Copy so each student has a card. Cut out each card along the dotted line.

Ⓢtudent Card

Life has its ups and downs. What has been the hardest time in your life?

Quotes & Statements

Ⓢtudent Card

What is it you like most about yourself? Why?

Quotes & Statements

Ⓢtudent Card

We all have good and bad habits. Talk about a good habit you have and how you can use it to make life better for someone else.

Quotes & Statements

Ⓢtudent Card

What is your greatest fear? How could you try to overcome it?

Quotes & Statements

Quotes & Statements
Discussion Cards *(continued)*

Directions: Copy so each student has a card. Cut out each card along the dotted line.

Student Card

When you think of heroes, who is your hero? Why is this individual a hero in your book?

Quotes & Statements

Student Card

Choose three adjectives to describe yourself and explain why you chose those descriptors.

Quotes & Statements

Student Card

Tell about a book you have read and what impact it had on who you are.

Quotes & Statements

Student Card

If you could choose to live anywhere, where would it be? Why?

Quotes & Statements

Quotes & Statements
Discussion Cards *(continued)*

Directions: Copy so each student has a card. Cut out each card along the dotted line.

Student Card

"I think adults really need to…"

Quotes & Statements

Student Card

"I think teachers really need to…"

Quotes & Statements

Student Card

"I think school should be…"

Quotes & Statements

Student Card

"My most embarassing moment happened when…"

Quotes & Statements

Quotes & Statements
Discussion Cards (continued)

Directions: Copy so each student has a card. Cut out each card along the dotted line.

Student Card

What type of career would you like to have? What will you do to prepare for it?

Quotes & Statements

Student Card

What is your favorite type of music and band? What do you like about the band's music?

Quotes & Statements

Student Card

How would you spend a day away from school?

Quotes & Statements

Student Card

What is one of your pet peeves? Why does this pet peeve bother you?

Quotes & Statements

Quotes & Statements
Discussion Cards (continued)

Directions: Copy so each student has a card. Cut out each card along the dotted line.

Student Card

It has been said that what we eat is what we are, and what we think is what we become.

Do you agree or disagree? Why?

Quotes & Statements

Student Card

Why is it important for cultural groups to maintain their heritage?

Quotes & Statements

Student Card

"The roots of education are bitter, but the fruit is sweet."

—*Aristotle*

What do you think Aristotle meant by this?

Quotes & Statements

Student Card

"Do something for someone everyday for which you don't get paid."

—*Albert Schweitzer*

What kindness can you do to make someone's life easier?

Quotes & Statements

Borrowed Words

Directions: Copy one set of cards per team. Cut out each card along the dotted line. Fold each card along the solid line so you have the question on one side and the answer on the other. Cards may be glued or taped to keep questions and answers on opposite sides. Students should keep answer section hidden.

Question 1	**Answer** 1
a la carte 1. What does it mean? 2. What language is it borrowed from? *Borrowed Words*	1. **Meaning:** items priced separately on menu 2. **Language:** French *Borrowed Words*
Question 2	**Answer** 2
alfresco 1. What does it mean? 2. What language is it borrowed from? *Borrowed Words*	1. **Meaning:** outdoor 2. **Language:** Italian *Borrowed Words*
Question 3	**Answer** 3
au revoir 1. What does it mean? 2. What language is it borrowed from? *Borrowed Words*	1. **Meaning:** good-bye, farewell 2. **Language:** French *Borrowed Words*
Question 4	**Answer** 4
bon voyage 1. What does it mean? 2. What language is it borrowed from? *Borrowed Words*	1. **Meaning:** have a good journey 2. **Language:** French *Borrowed Words*
Question 5	**Answer** 5
bona fide 1. What does it mean? 2. What language is it borrowed from? *Borrowed Words*	1. **Meaning:** in good faith 2. **Language:** Latin *Borrowed Words*
Question 6	**Answer** 6
cul-de-sac 1. What does it mean? 2. What language is it borrowed from? *Borrowed Words*	1. **Meaning:** dead-end street 2. **Language:** French *Borrowed Words*

Borrowed Words (continued)

Directions: Copy one set of cards per team. Cut out each card along the dotted line. Fold each card along the solid line so you have the question on one side and the answer on the other. Cards may be glued or taped to keep questions and answers on opposite sides. Students should keep answer section hidden.

Question 7	Answer 7
faux pas 1. What does it mean? 2. What language is it borrowed from? *Borrowed Words*	1. **Meaning:** a social blunder 2. **Language:** French *Borrowed Words*

Question 8	Answer 8
modus operandi 1. What does it mean? 2. What language is it borrowed from? *Borrowed Words*	1. **Meaning:** method or procedure 2. **Language:** Latin *Borrowed Words*

Question 9	Answer 9
renaissance 1. What does it mean? 2. What language is it borrowed from? *Borrowed Words*	1. **Meaning:** rebirth 2. **Language:** French *Borrowed Words*

Question 10	Answer 10
prima donna 1. What does it mean? 2. What language is it borrowed from? *Borrowed Words*	1. **Meaning:** lead female singer in opera 2. **Language:** Italian *Borrowed Words*

Question 11	Answer 11
résumé 1. What does it mean? 2. What language is it borrowed from? *Borrowed Words*	1. **Meaning:** summary 2. **Language:** French *Borrowed Words*

Question 12	Answer 12
status quo 1. What does it mean? 2. What language is it borrowed from? *Borrowed Words*	1. **Meaning:** existing state of affairs 2. **Language:** Latin *Borrowed Words*

Borrowed Words *(continued)*

Directions: Copy one set of cards per team. Cut out each card along the dotted line. Fold each card along the solid line so you have the question on one side and the answer on the other. Cards may be glued or taped to keep questions and answers on opposite sides. Students should keep answer section hidden.

Question 13	Answer 13
cuisine 1. What does it mean? 2. What language is it borrowed from? *Borrowed Words*	1. **Meaning:** a style of cooking 2. **Language:** French *Borrowed Words*

Question 14	Answer 14
umbrella 1. What does it mean? 2. What language is it borrowed from? *Borrowed Words*	1. **Meaning:** a fabric shade for weather protection 2. **Language:** Italian *Borrowed Words*

Question 15	Answer 15
tornado 1. What does it mean? 2. What language is it borrowed from? *Borrowed Words*	1. **Meaning:** a violent, windy storm 2. **Language:** Spanish *Borrowed Words*

Question 16	Answer 16
origami 1. What does it mean? 2. What language is it borrowed from? *Borrowed Words*	1. **Meaning:** the art of paper folding 2. **Language:** Japanese *Borrowed Words*

Question 17	Answer 17
antique 1. What does it mean? 2. What language is it borrowed from? *Borrowed Words*	1. **Meaning:** old 2. **Language:** French *Borrowed Words*

Question 18	Answer 18
muffin 1. What does it mean? 2. What language is it borrowed from? *Borrowed Words*	1. **Meaning:** type of bread 2. **Language:** German *Borrowed Words*

Inside-Outside Circle

Blackline

Borrowed Words (continued)

Directions: Copy one set of cards per team. Cut out each card along the dotted line. Fold each card along the solid line so you have the question on one side and the answer on the other. Cards may be glued or taped to keep questions and answers on opposite sides. Students should keep answer section hidden.

Question 19	Answer 19
kindergarten 1. What does it mean? 2. What language is it borrowed from? *Borrowed Words*	1. **Meaning:** school for young children 2. **Language:** German *Borrowed Words*

Question 20	Answer 20
futon 1. What does it mean? 2. What language is it borrowed from? *Borrowed Words*	1. **Meaning:** type of mattress 2. **Language:** Japanese *Borrowed Words*

Question 21	Answer 21
confetti 1. What does it mean? 2. What language is it borrowed from? *Borrowed Words*	1. **Meaning:** small bits of colored paper 2. **Language:** Italian *Borrowed Words*

Question 22	Answer 22
coyote 1. What does it mean? 2. What language is it borrowed from? *Borrowed Words*	1. **Meaning:** wolf-like animal 2. **Language:** Spanish *Borrowed Words*

Question 23	Answer 23
bouquet 1. What does it mean? 2. What language is it borrowed from? *Borrowed Words*	1. **Meaning:** a bunch of flowers 2. **Language:** French *Borrowed Words*

Question 24	Answer 24
chauffeur 1. What does it mean? 2. What language is it borrowed from? *Borrowed Words*	1. **Meaning:** a hired driver 2. **Language:** French *Borrowed Words*

Borrowed Words *(continued)*

Directions: Copy one set of cards per team. Cut out each card along the dotted line. Fold each card along the solid line so you have the question on one side and the answer on the other. Cards may be glued or taped to keep questions and answers on opposite sides. Students should keep answer section hidden.

Question 25 **souvenir** 1. What does it mean? 2. What language is it borrowed from? *Borrowed Words*	**Answer** 25 1. **Meaning:** memory 2. **Language:** French *Borrowed Words*
Question 26 **et cetera** 1. What does it mean? 2. What language is it borrowed from? *Borrowed Words*	**Answer** 26 1. **Meaning:** and others of the same kind 2. **Language:** Latin *Borrowed Words*
Question 27 **vice versa** 1. What does it mean? 2. What language is it borrowed from? *Borrowed Words*	**Answer** 27 1. **Meaning:** conversely 2. **Language:** Latin *Borrowed Words*
Question 28 **elite** 1. What does it mean? 2. What language is it borrowed from? *Borrowed Words*	**Answer** 28 1. **Meaning:** best of a class 2. **Language:** French *Borrowed Words*
Question 29 **stampede** 1. What does it mean? 2. What language is it borrowed from? *Borrowed Words*	**Answer** 29 1. **Meaning:** to rush away in a panic 2. **Language:** Spanish *Borrowed Words*
Question 30 **espresso** 1. What does it mean? 2. What language is it borrowed from? *Borrowed Words*	**Answer** 30 1. **Meaning:** dark coffee 2. **Language:** Italian *Borrowed Words*

The Adventures of Tom Sawyer

Novel Review Teacher Questions

Directions: The following are a set of sample questions related to the novel, *The Adventures of Tom Sawyer,* by Mark Twain. These questions are provided as an example of how you can use Inside-Outside Circle and Timed Pair Share to promote review and thinking about a novel. You can use the same process with any novel or even with a chapter or assigned reading section. The teacher reads the question and indicates which partner shares first. Students answer using Timed Pair Share. In Timed Pair Share, Partner A shares for 30 seconds while Partner B listens. Then Partner B shares while Partner A listens.

The Adventures of Tom Sawyer
by
Mark Twain

1 Even though Tom and Huck feel the need to protect their own safety, what bothers them about the promise they have made to keep silent?

2 How does Potter treat Tom when he comes to visit him in his cell? Why does Tom feel especially miserable after this visit to Potter?

3 During Potter's trial, we are able to sense the audience is annoyed with Potter's lawyer. What is it that he seems to be doing? What seems to be his method of defense?

4 The defense then surprises those in the courtroom. What is the reaction in the courtroom when Tom takes the witness stand? How does the audience respond to this situation?

5 Tom and Huck are pleased with the turn of events for Potter. However, they realize their problems are not over. What do they fear?

6 If you were in Tom's and Huck's shoes, what would you have done to save Potter from sure death?

The Pearl
Novel Review Question Cards

Directions: Copy one set of cards per team. Cut out each card along the dotted line. Fold each card along the solid line so you have the question on one side and the answer on the other. Cards may be glued or taped to keep questions and answers on opposite sides. Students should keep answer section hidden.

Question 1

What is the setting of Steinbeck's novel, *The Pearl*?

The Pearl Question Cards

Answer 1

A remote village in Mexico in 1930 or earlier

The Pearl Question Cards

Question 2

What time of day does the novel begin?

The Pearl Question Cards

Answer 2

Early in the morning

The Pearl Question Cards

Question 3

What is the first song the reader hears?

The Pearl Question Cards

Answer 3

"The Song of Family".

The Pearl Question Cards

Question 4

Describe the house in which Kino and his family live.

The Pearl Question Cards

Answer 4

A one-room brush hut with a dirt floor and a small fire pit

The Pearl Question Cards

Question 5

Who are the three main characters?

The Pearl Question Cards

Answer 5

Kino, Juana, and Coyotito

The Pearl Question Cards

Question 6

Why does Steinbeck refer to the night air as "poisonous"?

The Pearl Question Cards

Answer 6

The night air symbolizes a time when bad things happen.

The Pearl Question Cards

The Pearl
Novel Review Question Cards *(continued)*

Directions: Copy one set of cards per team. Cut out each card along the dotted line. Fold each card along the solid line so you have the question on one side and the answer on the other. Cards may be glued or taped to keep questions and answers on opposite sides. Students should keep answer section hidden.

Question 7	Answer 7
Why is the canoe important to Kino? The Pearl *Question Cards*	It represents the past, his heritage, and his future. The Pearl *Question Cards*

Question 8	Answer 8
What two similes does the narrator use to describe the appearance and size of the pearl? The Pearl *Question Cards*	As perfect as the moon and as large as a seagull's egg The Pearl *Question Cards*

Question 9	Answer 9
The pearl buyers are only concerned about what? The Pearl *Question Cards*	How much money will be received from the sale of Kino's pearl The Pearl *Question Cards*

Question 10	Answer 10
When is the "Song of Evil" first heard? The Pearl *Question Cards*	It is heard when the scorpion is attacking Coyotito. The Pearl *Question Cards*

Question 11	Answer 11
What is the final offer the pearl buyers propose to Kino? The Pearl *Question Cards*	500 pesos The Pearl *Question Cards*

Question 12	Answer 12
Why does Kino believe he is inferior to the doctor? The Pearl *Question Cards*	Kino believes he is poor, uneducated, and of a different race. The Pearl *Question Cards*

The Pearl
Novel Review Question Cards *(continued)*

Directions: Copy one set of cards per team. Cut out each card along the dotted line. Fold each card along the solid line so you have the question on one side and the answer on the other. Cards may be glued or taped to keep questions and answers on opposite sides. Students should keep answer section hidden.

Question 13	**Answer** 13
Why is the destruction of Kino's boat a terrible act? The Pearl *Question Cards*	The boat cannot protect itself. The Pearl *Question Cards*
Question 14	**Answer** 14
What does Kino tell Juan Tomas that he believes the pearl has become? The Pearl *Question Cards*	It is my soul. The Pearl *Question Cards*
Question 15	**Answer** 15
Why are the pearl buyers excited about Kino's pearl? The Pearl *Question Cards*	They enjoy the "hunt" and thrill of arguing over prices to get this great pearl at the lowest price. The Pearl *Question Cards*
Question 16	**Answer** 16
How does Kino's view of the pearl change? The Pearl *Question Cards*	His view changes from seeing its beauty to seeing it as ugly when he sees it under the buyer's magnifying glass. The Pearl *Question Cards*
Question 17	**Answer** 17
What are Juana's objections to keeping the pearl? The Pearl *Question Cards*	The pearl is evil and will destroy them. She wants Kino to throw it away. The Pearl *Question Cards*
Question 18	**Answer** 18
What does the pearl symbolize? The Pearl *Question Cards*	It demonstrates the good and evil in everything. The Pearl *Question Cards*

The Pearl
Novel Review Question Cards *(continued)*

Directions: Copy one set of cards per team. Cut out each card along the dotted line. Fold each card along the solid line so you have the question on one side and the answer on the other. Cards may be glued or taped to keep questions and answers on opposite sides. Students should keep answer section hidden.

Question 19	Answer 19
Why does Kino reject the pearl buyers offer? The Pearl *Question Cards*	They do not offer a fair price. The Pearl *Question Cards*
Question 20 What is the doctor's attitude when Kino and Juana bring him their sick child? The Pearl *Question Cards*	**Answer 20** At first the doctor is insulting because they are of a lower class and cannot afford his services. Later when he realizes they have the pearl, he is eager to help. The Pearl *Question Cards*
Question 21 What do the thieves try to do to Kino twice? The Pearl *Question Cards*	**Answer 21** They try to steal the pearl. The Pearl *Question Cards*
Question 22 What happens when the three trackers pursue Kino's family in flight? The Pearl *Question Cards*	**Answer 22** They end up killing Coyotito. The Pearl *Question Cards*
Question 23 When Kino and Juana return to LaPaz, what are they carrying? The Pearl *Question Cards*	**Answer 23** They are carrying the dead body of Coyotito. The Pearl *Question Cards*
Question 24 In the end, what does Kino do with the pearl? The Pearl *Question Cards*	**Answer 24** Kino throws the pearl into the sea. The Pearl *Question Cards*

The Pearl
Novel Review Question Cards (continued)

Directions: Copy one set of cards per team. Cut out each card along the dotted line. Fold each card along the solid line so you have the question on one side and the answer on the other. Cards may be glued or taped to keep questions and answers on opposite sides. Students should keep answer section hidden.

Question 25	**Answer** 25
What types of conflict are evident in the novel? The Pearl *Question Cards*	**Internal conflicts within characters** **External conflicts between characters** **Conflict of man (characters) vs. society** **Conflict of man vs. the unknown** **Outside forces that the character cannot control** The Pearl *Question Cards*

Question 26	**Answer** 26
Why does Juana not believe her own remedy will heal Coyotito? The Pearl *Question Cards*	**Her remedy does not have a doctor's authority.** The Pearl *Question Cards*

Question 27	**Answer** 27
At his first encounter with the thieves, what does Kino still believe? The Pearl *Question Cards*	**Kino admires and still believes in the pearl.** The Pearl *Question Cards*

Question 28	**Answer** 28
What does the pearl demonstrate for Kino and Juana? The Pearl *Question Cards*	**It demonstrates that greed corrupts and destroys.** The Pearl *Question Cards*

Question 29	**Answer** 29
The Pearl *Question Cards*	The Pearl *Question Cards*

Question 30	**Answer** 30
The Pearl *Question Cards*	The Pearl *Question Cards*

Idioms

Directions: Copy one set of cards per team. Cut out each card along the dotted line. Fold each card along the solid line so you have the question on one side and the answer on the other. Cards may be glued or taped to keep questions and answers on opposite sides. Students should keep answer section hidden.

Question 1 *My mother has a green thumb.* **Explain the meaning.** *Idioms*	**Answer** 1 *My mother has a green thumb* means my mother is good at working with plants and they stay green and healthy. *Idioms*
Question 2 *A-OK* **Explain the meaning.** *Idioms*	**Answer** 2 If things are *A-OK*, they are absolutely fine. *Idioms*
Question 3 *A pretty penny* **Explain the meaning.** *Idioms*	**Answer** 3 If something costs *a pretty penny,* it is rather expensive. *Idioms*
Question 4 *Back to the salt mines* **Explain the meaning.** *Idioms*	**Answer** 4 *Back to the salt mines* means having to return to work. *Idioms*
Question 5 *Having a bad hair day* **Explain the meaning.** *Idioms*	**Answer** 5 *Having a bad hair day* means things are not going the way you had planned or would have liked. *Idioms*
Question 6 *People who live in glass houses should not throw stones.* **Explain the meaning.** *Idioms*	**Answer** 6 *People who live in glass houses should not throw stones* means we should not criticize others for faults we may have ourselves. *Idioms*

Idioms (continued)

Directions: Copy one set of cards per team. Cut out each card along the dotted line. Fold each card along the solid line so you have the question on one side and the answer on the other. Cards may be glued or taped to keep questions and answers on opposite sides. Students should keep answer section hidden.

Question 7	Answer 7
Their bark is worse than their bite. Explain the meaning. *Idioms*	If someone's *bark is worse than their bite*, they may get angry and shout, but not take any action. *Idioms*

Question 8	Answer 8
Beating swords into plowshares Explain the meaning. *Idioms*	If people *beat swords into plowshares*, they spend money on humanitarian reasons rather than spending it on weapons. *Idioms*

Question 9	Answer 9
A card up your sleeve Explain the meaning. *Idioms*	If you have *a card up your sleeve*, you have a surprise planned that you are keeping quiet until it is the right time to reveal it. *Idioms*

Question 10	Answer 10
A cat and dog life Explain the meaning. *Idioms*	If someone is leading *a cat and dog life*, they are someone who is always arguing. *Idioms*

Question 11	Answer 11
Caught with your hand in the cookie jar Explain the meaning. *Idioms*	Someone who is *caught with their hand in the cookie jar* is someone who is caught doing something wrong. *Idioms*

Question 12	Answer 12
Dead in the water Explain the meaning. *Idioms*	If something is *dead in the water* it means something isn't going anywhere or making any progress. *Idioms*

Idioms (continued)

Directions: Copy one set of cards per team. Cut out each card along the dotted line. Fold each card along the solid line so you have the question on one side and the answer on the other. Cards may be glued or taped to keep questions and answers on opposite sides. Students should keep answer section hidden.

Question 13	**Answer** 13
Dig way down deep Explain the meaning. *Idioms*	When someone *digs way down deep*, they look into their inner feelings to see how they feel about something. *Idioms*
Question 14	**Answer** 14
Every cloud has a silver lining. Explain the meaning. *Idioms*	If a *cloud has a silver lining* it means there is always something positive to draw from our experiences, even the bad ones. *Idioms*
Question 15	**Answer** 15
Face the music Explain the meaning. *Idioms*	If you have to *face the music* it means you must face the consequences for your actions, usually something that you did wrong. *Idioms*
Question 16	**Answer** 16
Feeling blue Explain the meaning. *Idioms*	*Feeling blue* means you are feeling down and are unhappy or depressed. *Idioms*
Question 17	**Answer** 17
A fish out of water Explain the meaning. *Idioms*	If you are *a fish out of water*, you are feeling uncomfortable in a new situation. *Idioms*
Question 18	**Answer** 18
Getting in on the ground floor Explain the meaning. *Idioms*	If you *get in on the ground floor*, you are getting in on a project at the beginning, before you know if it will be successful or not. *Idioms*

Idioms (continued)

Directions: Copy one set of cards per team. Cut out each card along the dotted line. Fold each card along the solid line so you have the question on one side and the answer on the other. Cards may be glued or taped to keep questions and answers on opposite sides. Students should keep answer section hidden.

Question 19	Answer 19
Getting your feet wet **Explain the meaning.** Idioms	*Getting your feet wet* means you have the opportunity to get experience doing something for the first time. Idioms

Question 20	Answer 20
Get your goat **Explain the meaning.** Idioms	To *get your goat* means something annoys you. Idioms

Question 21	Answer 21
Happy medium **Explain the meaning.** Idioms	*Happy medium* means you are reaching an agreement with someone or a decision about something. Idioms

Question 22	Answer 22
Head for the hills **Explain the meaning.** Idioms	To *head for the hills* means someone is running away from their problem. Idioms

Question 23	Answer 23
Icing on the cake **Explain the meaning.** Idioms	*Icing on the cake* refers to something good that happens in addition to something good that has already happened. Idioms

Question 24	Answer 24
To jump through hoops **Explain the meaning.** Idioms	*To jump through hoops* means to be willing to go to great lengths to do something well. Idioms

Idioms (continued)

Directions: Copy one set of cards per team. Cut out each card along the dotted line. Fold each card along the solid line so you have the question on one side and the answer on the other. Cards may be glued or taped to keep questions and answers on opposite sides. Students should keep answer section hidden.

Question 25 *Pass the hat* Explain the meaning. *Idioms*	**Answer** 25 To *pass the hat* means you ask people in a group to give you or an organization some money. *Idioms*
Question 26 *Blessing in disguise* Explain the meaning. *Idioms*	**Answer** 26 A *blessing in disguise* is something good that may come from a situation but may not seem so at the moment. *Idioms*
Question 27 *Against the clock* Explain the meaning. *Idioms*	**Answer** 27 *Against the clock* means you are feeling rushed and short on time. *Idioms*
Question 28 *Cut to the chase* Explain the meaning. *Idioms*	**Answer** 28 *Cut to the chase* means you should leave out all the unnecessary details and get to the point. *Idioms*
Question 29 *Finding your feet* Explain the meaning. *Idioms*	**Answer** 29 *Finding your feet* means to become more comfortable in what you are doing. *Idioms*
Question 30 *On pins and needles* Explain the meaning. *Idioms*	**Answer** 30 *On pins and needles* means you may feel anxious or nervous, especially when you are anticipating something. *Idioms*

Blank Cards Template

Teacher Directions: Use this blank card template to make your own cards for Inside-Outside Circle.

Ⓢtudent Card

Ⓢtudent Card

Ⓢtudent Card

Ⓢtudent Card

Blank Cards Template

Teacher Directions: Use this blank card template to make your own cards for Inside-Outside Circle.

Question	**Answer**
Question	**Answer**
Question	**Answer**
Question	**Answer**
Question	**Answer**
Question	**Answer**

Quiz-Quiz-Trade
Structure 3

Structure 3

Quiz-Quiz-Trade

Students quiz a partner, get quizzed by a partner, and then trade cards to repeat the process with a new partner.

Group Size
Whole Class

Steps

Setup: The teacher prepares a set of question cards for the class, or each student creates a question card.

1 **Students Pair Up**
The teacher tells students to "*Stand up, put a hand up, and pair up.*"

2 **Partner A Quizes**
Partner A quizzes Partner B, using his or her question card.

3 **Partner B Responds**
Partner B responds.

4 **Partner A Praises or Coaches**
Partner A praises Partner B if he or she answered correctly. If not, Partner A shows Partner B the correct answer and offers help.

5 **Switch Roles**
Partners switch roles.

6 **Trade Cards**
Partners trade cards and thank each other.

7 **Repeat**
Repeat steps 1–6 a number of times, each time with a new partner.

Tips
- If you don't have enough cards for every student, it is ok to give the same card to multiple students.
- If you have more cards than students, you can give some students more than one card to use.
- When played with cards, steps 3–6 are Quiz-Quiz-Trade (see pages 74–168 for an example).
- Laminate cards for future use.

Activities

Blank Quiz-Quiz-Trade
Cards Template...168

Literary Terms

Directions: Copy enough cards so each student receives a card. Cut out the cards on the dotted line. Fold cards on solid line and tape or glue the Question and Answer card back to back.

1 Question

What is *alliteration*?

Literary Terms

1 Answer

Alliteration is the repetition of consonant sounds at the beginning of words.

Literary Terms

2 Question

What is *allusion*?

Literary Terms

2 Answer

Allusion is the reference to a famous person, place, event, or other work of literature.

Literary Terms

3 Question

What is the role of the *antagonist* in a work of literature?

Literary Terms

3 Answer

The *antagonist* is the force working against the main character, the protagonist, in a literary work. It may be another character or a force of nature.

Literary Terms

4 Question

What is a *ballad*?

Literary Terms

4 Answer

A *ballad* is a narrative folk song.

Literary Terms

5 Question

What is the role of the *character* in a story?

Literary Terms

5 Answer

The role of the *character* is to serve as the person, animal, or imaginary creature that takes the part in the action of a literary work.

Literary Terms

6 Question

What is *characterization*?

Literary Terms

6 Answer

Characterization refers to the techniques a writer uses to create and develop a character.

Literary Terms

Literary Terms (continued)

Directions: Copy enough cards so each student receives a card. Cut out the cards on the dotted line. Fold cards on solid line and tape or glue the Question and Answer card back to back.

7 Question

Where would you find the *climax* in a story?

Literary Terms

7 Answer

The *climax* is the turning point or high point of interest in the plot of a story or play.

Literary Terms

8 Question

What is *dialogue*?

Literary Terms

8 Answer

Dialogue is the conversation between two or more characters and is often set apart by quotations.

Literary Terms

9 Question

What is a *stanza*?

Literary Terms

9 Answer

A *stanza* is the grouping of lines in poetry.

Literary Terms

10 Question

What is *imagery*?

Literary Terms

10 Answer

Imagery is the language in writing that evokes the five senses—seeing, touching, hearing, smelling, and tasting.

Literary Terms

11 Question

What is an *essay*?

Literary Terms

11 Answer

An *essay* is a short nonfiction work that deals with one subject.

Literary Terms

12 Question

What is *figurative language*?

Literary Terms

12 Answer

Figurative language goes beyond the dictionary meanings of words to create imagery and descriptions; three common forms are simile, metaphor, and personification.

Literary Terms

Literary Terms (continued)

Directions: Copy enough cards so each student receives a card. Cut out the cards on the dotted line. Fold cards on solid line and tape or glue the Question and Answer card back to back.

13 Question

What is *foreshadowing*?

Literary Terms

13 Answer

Foreshadowing is a writer's use of hints suggesting events that will occur later in the story.

Literary Terms

14 Question

What is *genre*?

Literary Terms

14 Answer

Genre is a term used to identify the major categories of literature; there are four main genres: fiction, nonfiction, poetry, and drama.

Literary Terms

15 Question

What is *hyperbole*?

Literary Terms

15 Answer

Hyperbole is a figure of speech that is an exaggerated description or statement.

Literary Terms

16 Question

What is *irony*?

Literary Terms

16 Answer

The contrast between what is expected and what actually exists or happens is called *irony*.

Literary Terms

17 Question

What is a *legend*?

Literary Terms

17 Answer

A *legend* is a story handed down from the past about a specific person, usually someone with heroic accomplishments.

Literary Terms

18 Question

What is a *metaphor*?

Literary Terms

18 Answer

A metaphor is the comparison of two unlike things that have something in common; it does not use the words *like* or *as*.

Literary Terms

Literary Terms *(continued)*

Directions: Copy enough cards so each student receives a card. Cut out the cards on the dotted line. Fold cards on solid line and tape or glue the Question and Answer card back to back.

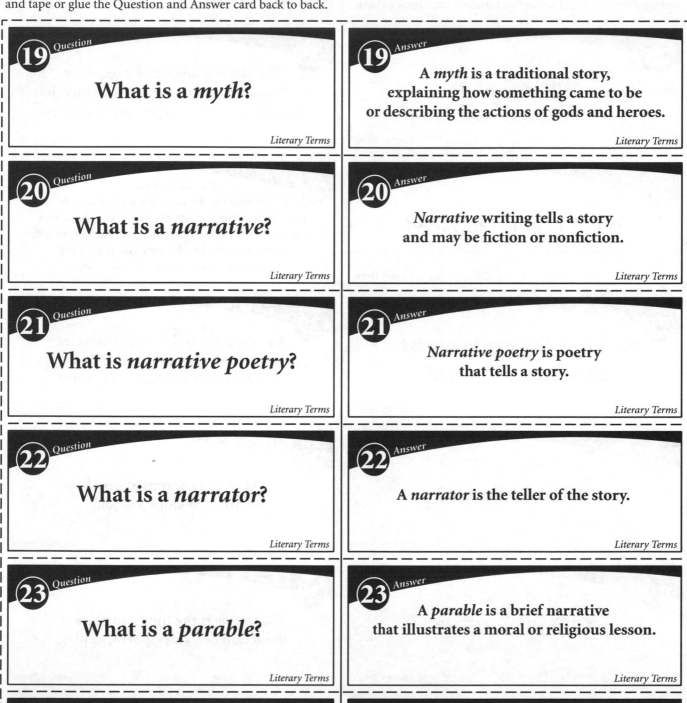

19 Question

What is a *myth*?

Literary Terms

19 Answer

A *myth* is a traditional story, explaining how something came to be or describing the actions of gods and heroes.

Literary Terms

20 Question

What is a *narrative*?

Literary Terms

20 Answer

Narrative writing tells a story and may be fiction or nonfiction.

Literary Terms

21 Question

What is *narrative poetry*?

Literary Terms

21 Answer

Narrative poetry is poetry that tells a story.

Literary Terms

22 Question

What is a *narrator*?

Literary Terms

22 Answer

A *narrator* is the teller of the story.

Literary Terms

23 Question

What is a *parable*?

Literary Terms

23 Answer

A *parable* is a brief narrative that illustrates a moral or religious lesson.

Literary Terms

24 Question

What is *personification*?

Literary Terms

24 Answer

The giving of human qualities to an animal, object, or idea is called *personification*.

Literary Terms

Literary Terms (continued)

Directions: Copy enough cards so each student receives a card. Cut out the cards on the dotted line. Fold cards on solid line and tape or glue the Question and Answer card back to back.

25 Question

What is *plot*?

Literary Terms

25 Answer

The *plot* is made up of a sequence of related events that complete a story; it is the action, or what happens in the story.

Literary Terms

26 Question

What is *point of view*?

Literary Terms

26 Answer

Point of view is the perspective from which a story is told. First person: the narrator is one of the characters and uses pronouns such as *I, me, we*. Third person: the narrator is not in the story and relates the story using pronouns such as *he, she, it*.

Literary Terms

27 Question

Who is the *protagonist* in a literary work?

Literary Terms

27 Answer

A *protagonist* is the main character in a literary work. A *protagonist* is always involved in the conflict of the story.

Literary Terms

28 Question

What is *rhyme*?

Literary Terms

28 Answer

Rhyme is the repetition of identical or similar sounds.

Literary Terms

29 Question

What is *setting*?

Literary Terms

29 Answer

The *setting* is the time and place of the action of a story, poem, or play.

Literary Terms

30 Question

What is a *short story*?

Literary Terms

30 Answer

A *short story* is a work of fiction that can generally be read in one sitting.

Literary Terms

Literary Terms (continued)

Directions: Copy enough cards so each student receives a card. Cut out the cards on the dotted line. Fold cards on solid line and tape or glue the Question and Answer card back to back.

31 Question

What is a *simile*?

Literary Terms

31 Answer

A *simile* is a comparison of two unlike things that have some quality in common; it uses *like* or *as*, and makes a direct comparison.

Literary Terms

32 Question

What is a *symbol*?

Literary Terms

32 Answer

A *symbol* is a person, place, object, or action that stands for something outside of itself.

Literary Terms

33 Question

What is *theme*?

Literary Terms

33 Answer

The *theme* is the message about life or human nature communicated by a work of literature.

Literary Terms

34 Question

What is *analogy*?

Literary Terms

34 Answer

Analogy is a comparison of two pairs that have the same relationship.

Literary Terms

35 Question

What is *motif*?

Literary Terms

35 Answer

Motif is the recurring structures, contrasts, or literary devices that can help develop a text's major themes.

Literary Terms

36 Question

What is *tone*?

Literary Terms

36 Answer

Tone is the writer's mood or attitude toward his or her readers as seen through the characters.

Literary Terms

Literary Terms *(continued)*

Directions: Copy enough cards so each student receives a card. Cut out the cards on the dotted line. Fold cards on solid line and tape or glue the Question and Answer card back to back.

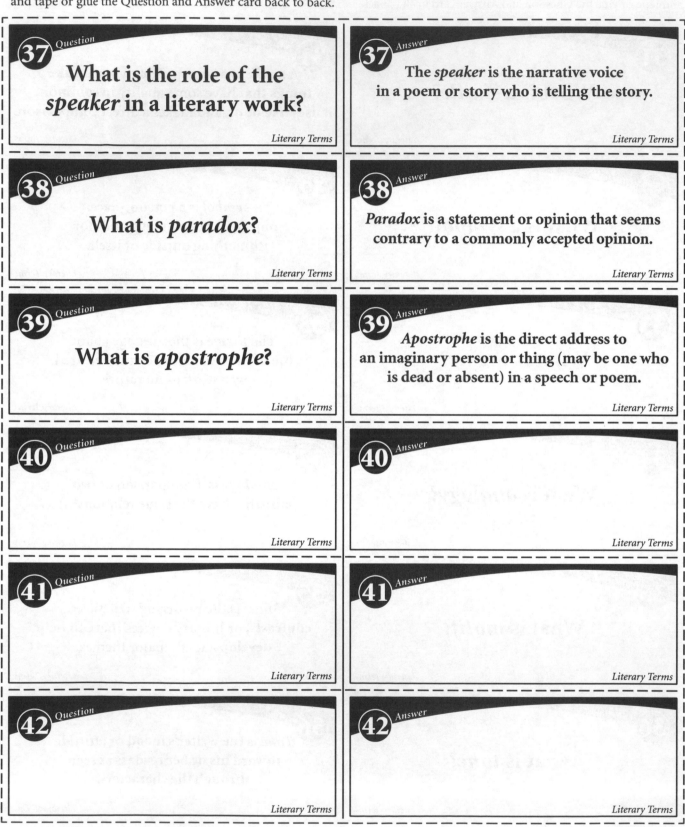

37 Question

What is the role of the *speaker* in a literary work?

Literary Terms

37 Answer

The *speaker* is the narrative voice in a poem or story who is telling the story.

Literary Terms

38 Question

What is *paradox*?

Literary Terms

38 Answer

Paradox is a statement or opinion that seems contrary to a commonly accepted opinion.

Literary Terms

39 Question

What is *apostrophe*?

Literary Terms

39 Answer

Apostrophe is the direct address to an imaginary person or thing (may be one who is dead or absent) in a speech or poem.

Literary Terms

40 Question

Literary Terms

40 Answer

Literary Terms

41 Question

Literary Terms

41 Answer

Literary Terms

42 Question

Literary Terms

42 Answer

Literary Terms

Julius Caesar
Character Cards

Directions: Copy enough cards so each student receives a card. Cut out the cards on the dotted line. Fold cards on solid line and tape or glue the Question and Answer card back to back.

① Question

Who is Julius Caesar?

Julius Caesar Character Cards

① Answer
- Emperor of Rome
- Wants to be king of Rome
- Assassinated midway through play

Julius Caesar Character Cards

② Question

Who is Casca?

Julius Caesar Character Cards

② Answer
- Aids in conspiracy to assassinate Caesar
- First to stab Caesar

Julius Caesar Character Cards

③ Question

Who is Calpurnia?

Julius Caesar Character Cards

③ Answer
- Caesar's wife
- Suspicious of events
- Dreams Caesar is murdered
- Tries to divert assassination

Julius Caesar Character Cards

④ Question

Who is Marcus Antonius?

Julius Caesar Character Cards

④ Answer
- Pretends to be friend and confidant to Caesar
- Skilled orator
- He and Octavius defeat Brutus and Cassius at Philippi

Julius Caesar Character Cards

⑤ Question

Who is the Soothsayer?

Julius Caesar Character Cards

⑤ Answer
- Warns Caesar at celebration of Feast of Lupercal to "beware the Ides of March"
- Warns Caesar again as he enters Senate House

Julius Caesar Character Cards

⑥ Question

Who is Marcus Brutus?

Julius Caesar Character Cards

⑥ Answer
- Judicial magistrate of Rome
- Joins the conspiracy
- Commits suicide rather than be taken prisoner

Julius Caesar Character Cards

Julius Caesar
Character Cards (continued)

Directions: Copy enough cards so each student receives a card. Cut out the cards on the dotted line. Fold cards on solid line and tape or glue the Question and Answer card back to back.

 7 Question

Who is Cassius?

Julius Caesar Character Cards

 7 Answer

- **Brother-in-law to Brutus**
- **Organizes the conspiracy against Caesar**
- **Commits suicide when he "thinks" Brutus has been defeated**

Julius Caesar Character Cards

 8 Question

Who is Cicero?

Julius Caesar Character Cards

 8 Answer

- **Senator and famous orator of Rome**
- **Philosophical type of character**

Julius Caesar Character Cards

 9 Question

Who is Cinna?

Julius Caesar Character Cards

 9 Answer

- **Conspirator**
- **Wants Cassius to get Brutus to help in conspiracy**
- **Places Cassius's forged letters for Brutus to find**

Julius Caesar Character Cards

 10 Question

Who is Lucius?

Julius Caesar Character Cards

 10 Answer

- **Brutus's young servant**
- **Brutus treats him with kindness and understanding**

Julius Caesar Character Cards

 11 Question

Who is Decius Brutus?

Julius Caesar Character Cards

 11 Answer

- **Conspirator**
- **Persuades Caesar to attend Senate on the Ides of March**
- **Tells Caesar the Senate intends to crown him as king**

Julius Caesar Character Cards

 12 Question

Who is Metellus Cimber?

Julius Caesar Character Cards

 12 Answer

- **Conspirator**
- **Helps assassins to surround Caesar**
- **Manipulates event so Casca can stab Caesar from behind**

Julius Caesar Character Cards

Julius Caesar
Character Cards (continued)

Directions: Copy enough cards so each student receives a card. Cut out the cards on the dotted line. Fold cards on solid line and tape or glue the Question and Answer card back to back.

13 *Question*

Who is Portia?

Julius Caesar *Character Cards*

13 *Answer*
- Wife of Brutus
- Knows Brutus plans to assassinate Caesar
- Commits suicide when she realizes Brutus is doomed

Julius Caesar *Character Cards*

14 *Question*

Who is Caius Ligarius?

Julius Caesar *Character Cards*

14 *Answer*
- Final member of conspiracy group
- Pretends to be ill on assassination day
- Later says he's better and will do whatever Brutus wants

Julius Caesar *Character Cards*

15 *Question*

Who is Publius?

Julius Caesar *Character Cards*

15 *Answer*
- Elderly senator
- Comes with conspirators to escort Caesar to Capitol
- Witnesses assassination
- Brutus gets Publius to tell citizens no one else will be harmed

Julius Caesar *Character Cards*

16 *Question*

Who is Artemidorus?

Julius Caesar *Character Cards*

16 *Answer*
- Gives Caesar a letter when emperor enters Capitol
- Letter identifies conspirators and the plan to kill him
- Caesar never reads the letter

Julius Caesar *Character Cards*

17 *Question*

Who is Popilius Lena?

Julius Caesar *Character Cards*

17 *Answer*
- Senator who wishes Cassius well as Caesar enters Senate House

Julius Caesar *Character Cards*

18 *Question*

Who is M. Aemilius Lepidus?

Julius Caesar *Character Cards*

18 *Answer*
- Joins Antony and Octavius to form second Triumvirate after Caesar's assassination
- Weak individual
- Errand runner for Antony

Julius Caesar *Character Cards*

Julius Caesar
Character Cards (continued)

Directions: Copy enough cards so each student receives a card. Cut out the cards on the dotted line. Fold cards on solid line and tape or glue the Question and Answer card back to back.

---

19 Question

Who is Lucilius?

Julius Caesar Character Cards

19 Answer
- Impersonates Brutus at the second battle of Philippi
- Captured by Antony's soldiers
- Antony admires his loyalty to Brutus and protects him *Julius Caesar Character Cards*

---

20 Question

Who is Pindarus?

Julius Caesar Character Cards

20 Answer
- Lies about Titinius being captured by the enemy
- Cassius has Pindarus kill him with sword used to kill Caesar

Julius Caesar Character Cards

---

21 Question

Who is Titinius?

Julius Caesar Character Cards

21 Answer
- Officer in the army commanded by Cassius and Brutus
- Guards tent at Sardis while the two generals argue
- Commits suicide because Cassius did so *Julius Caesar Character Cards*

---

22 Question

Who are Varro and Claudius?

Julius Caesar Character Cards

22 Answer
- Servants of Brutus
- Spend the night in Brutus's tent at Sardis
- Neither see the ghost of Caesar that appears to Brutus *Julius Caesar Character Cards*

---

23 Question

Who is Young Cato?

Julius Caesar Character Cards

23 Answer
- Son of Marcus Cato
- Brother of Portia
- Soldier in the army commanded by Brutus and Cassius
- Dies in second battle at Philippi *Julius Caesar Character Cards*

---

24 Question

Who are Clitus and Dardanius?

Julius Caesar Character Cards

24 Answer
- Servants of Brutus
- Refuse to kill Brutus when he requests they do so

Julius Caesar Character Cards

Julius Caesar
Character Cards *(continued)*

Directions: Copy enough cards so each student receives a card. Cut out the cards on the dotted line. Fold cards on solid line and tape or glue the Question and Answer card back to back.

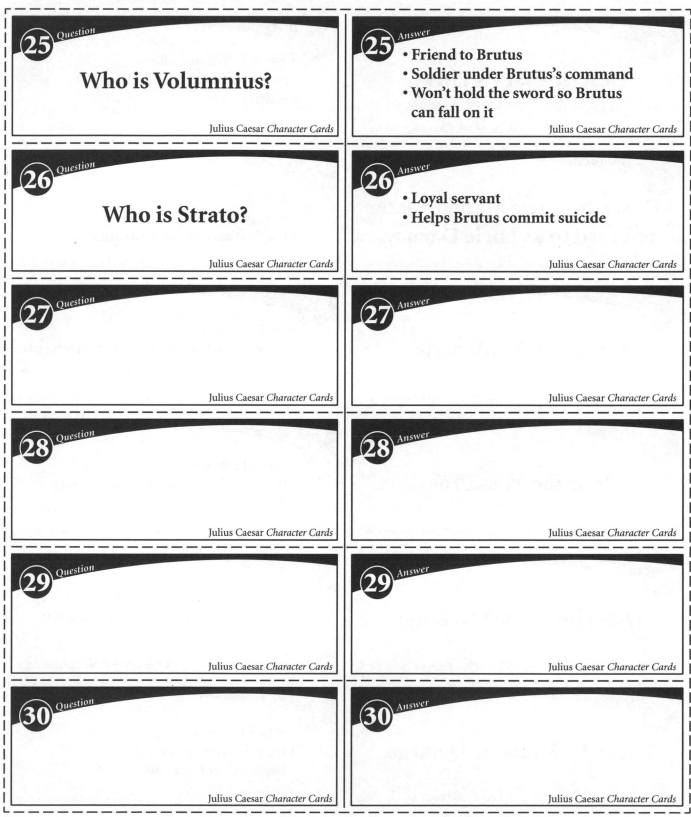

25 Question

Who is Volumnius?

Julius Caesar Character Cards

25 Answer

• **Friend to Brutus**
• **Soldier under Brutus's command**
• **Won't hold the sword so Brutus can fall on it**

Julius Caesar Character Cards

26 Question

Who is Strato?

Julius Caesar Character Cards

26 Answer

• **Loyal servant**
• **Helps Brutus commit suicide**

Julius Caesar Character Cards

27 Question

Julius Caesar Character Cards

27 Answer

Julius Caesar Character Cards

28 Question

Julius Caesar Character Cards

28 Answer

Julius Caesar Character Cards

29 Question

Julius Caesar Character Cards

29 Answer

Julius Caesar Character Cards

30 Question

Julius Caesar Character Cards

30 Answer

Julius Caesar Character Cards

A Tale of Two Cities
Character Cards

Directions: Copy enough cards so each student receives a card. Cut out the cards on the dotted line. Fold cards on solid line and tape or glue the Question and Answer card back to back.

1 Question

Describe Jarvis Lorry.

A Tale of Two Cities *Character Cards*

1 Answer

- Agent in Tellson's Bank
- Befriends the Manettes
- Elderly

A Tale of Two Cities *Character Cards*

2 Question

Describe Lucie Manette, later referred to as Lucie Darnay.

A Tale of Two Cities *Character Cards*

2 Answer

- Young
- Compassionate
- Inspiration and loyal to others

A Tale of Two Cities *Character Cards*

3 Question

Describe Dr. Manette.

A Tale of Two Cities *Character Cards*

3 Answer

- Lucie's father
- Prisoner in the Bastille for eighteen years

A Tale of Two Cities *Character Cards*

4 Question

Describe Miss Pross.

A Tale of Two Cities *Character Cards*

4 Answer

- Englishwoman
- Works as Lucie's nurse and protector

A Tale of Two Cities *Character Cards*

5 Question

Describe Ernest Defarge.

A Tale of Two Cities *Character Cards*

5 Answer

- Owner of wine shop in Paris
- Becomes leader in French Revolution

A Tale of Two Cities *Character Cards*

6 Question

Describe Madame Defarge.

A Tale of Two Cities *Character Cards*

6 Answer

- Wife of Ernest
- Despises the upper class
- Force behind Revolution

A Tale of Two Cities *Character Cards*

A Tale of Two Cities
Character Cards (continued)

Directions: Copy enough cards so each student receives a card. Cut out the cards on the dotted line. Fold cards on solid line and tape or glue the Question and Answer card back to back.

---

7 Question

Describe the "Jacques".

A Tale of Two Cities *Character Cards*

---

7 Answer

• Secret group of revolutionaries

A Tale of Two Cities *Character Cards*

---

8 Question

Describe Jeremy (Jerry) Cruncher.

A Tale of Two Cities *Character Cards*

---

8 Answer

• Porter at Tellson's
• Jarvis's errand man
• Secretly serves as a body snatcher

A Tale of Two Cities *Character Cards*

---

9 Question

Describe Mrs. Cruncher.

A Tale of Two Cities *Character Cards*

---

9 Answer

• Jerry's wife
• Pious woman
• Often beaten by her husband for praying

A Tale of Two Cities *Character Cards*

---

10 Question

Describe Sydney Carton.

A Tale of Two Cities *Character Cards*

---

10 Answer

• Lawyer
• Heavy drinker
• Looks like a double for Charles Darnay

A Tale of Two Cities *Character Cards*

---

11 Question

Describe C. J. Stryver.

A Tale of Two Cities *Character Cards*

---

11 Answer

• Darnay's defense lawyer in England
• Sydney Carton's employer

A Tale of Two Cities *Character Cards*

---

12 Question

Describe Roger Cly.

A Tale of Two Cities *Character Cards*

---

12 Answer

• Police spy in England
• Betrays Darnay
• Becomes a prison spy in Revolutionary France

A Tale of Two Cities *Character Cards*

A Tale of Two Cities
Character Cards *(continued)*

Directions: Copy enough cards so each student receives a card. Cut out the cards on the dotted line. Fold cards on solid line and tape or glue the Question and Answer card back to back.

---

13 Question

Describe John Barsad.

A Tale of Two Cities Character Cards

13 Answer
- Also known as Solomon Pross
- Police spy in England
- Betrays Darnay
- Becomes a prison spy in Revolutionary France
- Helps Carton save Darnay

A Tale of Two Cities Character Cards

---

14 Question

Describe Monseigneur the Marquis.

A Tale of Two Cities Character Cards

14 Answer
- Greedy French aristocrat
- His belongings are confiscated during the Revolution

A Tale of Two Cities Character Cards

---

15 Question

Describe Marquis St. Evrémonde.

A Tale of Two Cities Character Cards

15 Answer
- Darnay's wicked uncle who is murdered by a revolutionist

A Tale of Two Cities Character Cards

---

16 Question

Describe Gabelle.

A Tale of Two Cities Character Cards

16 Answer
- Local tax collector
- Works for Evrémonde family

A Tale of Two Cities Character Cards

---

17 Question

Describe Gaspard.

A Tale of Two Cities Character Cards

17 Answer
- Assassin of Marquis St. Evrémonde because Marquis ran his child down

A Tale of Two Cities Character Cards

---

18 Question

Describe Road-mender and Wood-sawyer.

A Tale of Two Cities Character Cards

18 Answer
- Man initiated into the Revolutionary Movement by Defarge
- Becomes a bloodthirsty revolutionist

A Tale of Two Cities Character Cards

A Tale of Two Cities
Character Cards *(continued)*

Directions: Copy enough cards so each student receives a card. Cut out the cards on the dotted line. Fold cards on solid line and tape or glue the Question and Answer card back to back.

19 Question

Describe the young Lucie Darnay.

A Tale of Two Cities Character Cards

19 Answer

- Child of Lucie and Charles Darnay
- Is taken to France during Reign of Terror
- Father is imprisoned there

A Tale of Two Cities Character Cards

20 Question

Describe Foulon.

A Tale of Two Cities Character Cards

20 Answer

- Arrogant aristocrat
- Hanged after storming of the Bastille

A Tale of Two Cities Character Cards

21 Question

Describe Vengeance.

A Tale of Two Cities Character Cards

21 Answer

- A murderous revolutionist
- Becomes the henchman for Madame Defarge

A Tale of Two Cities Character Cards

22 Question

Describe the Seamstress.

A Tale of Two Cities Character Cards

22 Answer

- Pathetic young woman
- Executed with Darnay

A Tale of Two Cities Character Cards

23 Question

A Tale of Two Cities Character Cards

23 Answer

A Tale of Two Cities Character Cards

24 Question

A Tale of Two Cities Character Cards

24 Answer

A Tale of Two Cities Character Cards

Confused Words

Directions: Copy enough cards so each student receives a card. Cut out the cards on the dotted line. Fold cards on solid line and tape or glue the Question and Answer card back to back.

1 Question
How are these words different in meaning?

1. Accept
2. Except

Confused Words

1 Answer
1. Accept: to receive
2. Except: to leave out

Confused Words

2 Question
How are these words different in meaning?

1. Allusion
2. Illusion

Confused Words

2 Answer
1. Allusion: an indirect reference
2. Illusion: a false view of reality

Confused Words

3 Question
How are these words different in meaning?

1. Altogether
2. All together

Confused Words

3 Answer
1. Altogether: entirely
2. All together: everything is in one place

Confused Words

4 Question
How are these words different in meaning?

1. Ascent
2. Assent

Confused Words

4 Answer
1. Ascent: to climb
2. Assent: agreement

Confused Words

5 Question
How are these words different in meaning?

1. Capital
2. Capitol

Confused Words

5 Answer
1. Capital: seat in government
2. Capitol: building where legislature meets

Confused Words

6 Question
How are these words different in meaning?

1. Complement
2. Compliment

Confused Words

6 Answer
1. Complement: something that completes something else
2. Compliment: praising or thanking

Confused Words

Confused Words (continued)

Directions: Copy enough cards so each student receives a card. Cut out the cards on the dotted line. Fold cards on solid line and tape or glue the Question and Answer card back to back.

---

 7 Question

How are these words different in meaning?

1. Council

2. Counsel

Confused Words

---

 7 Answer

1. Council: group that advises
2. Counsel: to advise others

Confused Words

---

 8 Question

How are these words different in meaning?

1. Eminent

2. Imminent

Confused Words

---

 8 Answer

1. Eminent: famous or respected
2. Imminent: ready to happen

Confused Words

---

 9 Question

How are these words different in meaning?

1. A lot

2. Alot

Confused Words

---

 9 Answer

1. A lot: two words meaning many
2. Alot: not a word, never a correct form

Confused Words

---

 10 Question

How are these words different in meaning?

1. All ready

2. Already

Confused Words

---

 10 Answer

1. All ready: something that is prepared
2. Already: by this time

Confused Words

---

 11 Question

How are these words different in meaning?

1. Apart

2. A part

Confused Words

---

 11 Answer

1. Apart: being separated
2. A part: being joined with something

Confused Words

---

 12 Question

How are these words different in meaning?

1. Breath

2. Breathe

Confused Words

---

 12 Answer

1. Breath: air inhaled or exhaled
2. Breathe: to inhale or exhale

Confused Words

Confused Words (continued)

Directions: Copy enough cards so each student receives a card. Cut out the cards on the dotted line. Fold cards on solid line and tape or glue the Question and Answer card back to back.

---

13 Question
How are these words different in meaning?

1. Cite

2. Site

Confused Words

13 Answer
1. Cite: to quote or document information
2. Site: location, place, or position

Confused Words

---

14 Question
How are these words different in meaning?

1. Conscience

2. Conscious

Confused Words

14 Answer
1. Conscience: a sense of right and wrong
2. Conscious: to be awake

Confused Words

---

15 Question
How are these words different in meaning?

1. Elicit

2. Illicit

Confused Words

15 Answer
1. Elicit: to draw or bring out information from an individual
2. Illicit: something illegal

Confused Words

---

16 Question
How are these words different in meaning?

1. Its

2. It's

Confused Words

16 Answer
1. Its: belonging to "it"
2. It's: contraction meaning *it is*

Confused Words

---

17 Question
How are these words different in meaning?

1. Lead

2. Led

Confused Words

17 Answer
1. Lead: a piece of metal (noun)
2. Led: to guide, past tense of *to lead* (verb)

Confused Words

---

18 Question
How are these words different in meaning?

1. Lose

2. Loose

Confused Words

18 Answer
1. Lose: not winning or to misplace something
2. Loose: not tight

Confused Words

Confused Words (continued)

Directions: Copy enough cards so each student receives a card. Cut out the cards on the dotted line. Fold cards on solid line and tape or glue the Question and Answer card back to back.

19 *Question*
How are these words different in meaning?
1. Passed
2. Past
Confused Words

19 *Answer*
1. *Passed:* moved, past tense of *to pass*
2. *Past:* a former time or location
Confused Words

20 *Question*
How are these words different in meaning?
1. Piece
2. Peace
Confused Words

20 *Answer*
1. *Piece:* a part of something
2. *Peace:* agreement about an issue or a feeling of contentment
Confused Words

21 *Question*
How are these words different in meaning?
1. Precede
2. Proceed
Confused Words

21 *Answer*
1. *Precede:* to come before something
2. *Proceed:* to go forward
Confused Words

22 *Question*
How are these words different in meaning?
1. Principal
2. Principle
Confused Words

22 *Answer*
1. *Principal:* person of authority
2. *Principle:* a basic truth
Confused Words

23 *Question*
How are these words different in meaning?
1. Stationary
2. Stationery
Confused Words

23 *Answer*
1. *Stationary:* stopping, standing still
2. *Stationery:* writing paper
Confused Words

24 *Question*
How are these words different in meaning?
1. Suppose
2. Supposed
Confused Words

24 *Answer*
1. *Suppose:* to make a guess
2. *Supposed:* obligated to do something
Confused Words

Confused Words *(continued)*

Directions: Copy enough cards so each student receives a card. Cut out the cards on the dotted line. Fold cards on solid line and tape or glue the Question and Answer card back to back.

25 Question

How are these words different in meaning?

1. Than
2. Then

Confused Words

25 Answer

1. Than: used when making comparisons
2. Then: at that time, or next in a series

Confused Words

26 Question

How are these words different in meaning?

1. Their
2. There
3. They're

Confused Words

26 Answer

1. Their: belonging to
2. There: a place or location
3. They're: contraction meaning *they are*

Confused Words

27 Question

How are these words different in meaning?

1. To
2. Too
3. Two

Confused Words

27 Answer

1. To: direction, go to or toward something
2. Too: also, too much
3. Two: the number

Confused Words

28 Question

How are these words different in meaning?

1. Who
2. Which
3. That

Confused Words

28 Answer

1. Who: a reference to a
person or persons
2. Which: a reference to a thing
3. That: a reference to things or
a group of something

Confused Words

29 Question

How are these words different in meaning?

1. Who
2. Whom

Confused Words

29 Answer

1. Who: used as a subject
2. Whom: used as an object

Confused Words

30 Question

Confused Words

30 Answer

Confused Words

Latin Root
Word Meanings and Examples

Directions: Copy enough cards so each student receives a card. Cut out the cards on the dotted line. Fold cards on solid line and tape or glue the Question and Answer card back to back.

1 Question

Latin Root: *dict*
Meaning: *to say*
What words are examples for this root?

Latin Root Word Meanings and Examples

1 Answer

Examples:
• Dictate
• Predict

Latin Root Word Meanings and Examples

2 Question

Latin Root: *duc*
Meaning: *to lead, bring, or take*
What words are examples for this root?

Latin Root Word Meanings and Examples

2 Answer

Examples:
• Deduce
• Reduce

Latin Root Word Meanings and Examples

3 Question

Latin Root: *gress*
Meaning: *to walk*
What words are examples for this root?

Latin Root Word Meanings and Examples

3 Answer

Examples:
• Digress
• Transgress

Latin Root Word Meanings and Examples

4 Question

Latin Root: *ject*
Meaning: *to throw*
What words are examples for this root?

Latin Root Word Meanings and Examples

4 Answer

Examples:
• Project
• Reject

Latin Root Word Meanings and Examples

5 Question

Latin Root: *pel*
Meaning: *to drive*
What words are examples for this root?

Latin Root Word Meanings and Examples

5 Answer

Examples:
• Compel
• Dispel

Latin Root Word Meanings and Examples

6 Question

Latin Root: *pend*
Meaning: *to hang*
What words are examples for this root?

Latin Root Word Meanings and Examples

6 Answer

Examples:
• Depend
• Pendulum

Latin Root Word Meanings and Examples

Latin Root
Word Meanings and Examples *(continued)*

Directions: Copy enough cards so each student receives a card. Cut out the cards on the dotted line. Fold cards on solid line and tape or glue the Question and Answer card back to back.

7 Question
Latin Root: *port*
Meaning: *to carry*
What words are examples for this root?
Latin Root Word Meanings and Examples

7 Answer
Examples:
• Deport
• Support
Latin Root Word Meanings and Examples

8 Question
Latin Root: *scribe/script*
Meaning: *to write*
What words are examples for this root?
Latin Root Word Meanings and Examples

8 Answer
Examples:
• Describe
• Transcription
Latin Root Word Meanings and Examples

9 Question
Latin Root: *tract*
Meaning: *to pull or draw*
What words are examples for this root?
Latin Root Word Meanings and Examples

9 Answer
Examples:
• Attract
• Extract
Latin Root Word Meanings and Examples

10 Question
Latin Root: *sta*
Meaning: *to stand*
What words are examples for this root?
Latin Root Word Meanings and Examples

10 Answer
Examples:
• Statute
• Constable
Latin Root Word Meanings and Examples

11 Question
Latin Root: *pli*
Meaning: *to fold*
What words are examples for this root?
Latin Root Word Meanings and Examples

11 Answer
Examples:
• Accomplice
• Complicity
Latin Root Word Meanings and Examples

12 Question
Latin Root: *jur*
Meaning: *right*
What words are examples for this root?
Latin Root Word Meanings and Examples

12 Answer
Examples:
• Jurisdiction
• Perjury
Latin Root Word Meanings and Examples

Latin Root
Word Meanings and Examples *(continued)*

Directions: Copy enough cards so each student receives a card. Cut out the cards on the dotted line. Fold cards on solid line and tape or glue the Question and Answer card back to back.

---

13 Question

Latin Root: *cred*
Meaning: *to trust*
What words are examples for this root?

Latin Root Word Meanings and Examples

---

13 Answer

Examples:
• Credible
• Discredit

Latin Root Word Meanings and Examples

---

14 Question

Latin Root: *fut*
Meaning: *to disprove*
What words are examples for this root?

Latin Root Word Meanings and Examples

---

14 Answer

Examples:
• Refute
• Futile

Latin Root Word Meanings and Examples

---

15 Question

Latin Root: *proto*
Meaning: *first*
What words are examples for this root?

Latin Root Word Meanings and Examples

---

15 Answer

Examples:
• Prototype
• Protocol

Latin Root Word Meanings and Examples

---

16 Question

Latin Root: *sue*
Meaning: *to follow*
What words are examples for this root?

Latin Root Word Meanings and Examples

---

16 Answer

Examples:
• Ensue
• Pursue

Latin Root Word Meanings and Examples

---

17 Question

Latin Root: *err*
Meaning: *to wander*
What words are examples for this root?

Latin Root Word Meanings and Examples

---

17 Answer

Examples:
• Erratic
• Errant

Latin Root Word Meanings and Examples

---

18 Question

Latin Root: *pla*
Meaning: *to please*
What words are examples for this root?

Latin Root Word Meanings and Examples

---

18 Answer

Examples:
• Platitude
• Complacent

Latin Root Word Meanings and Examples

Latin Root
Word Meanings and Examples (continued)

Directions: Copy enough cards so each student receives a card. Cut out the cards on the dotted line. Fold cards on solid line and tape or glue the Question and Answer card back to back.

---

19 Question

Latin Root: *vert*
Meaning: *to turn*
What words are examples for this root?

Latin Root Word Meanings and Examples

19 Answer

Examples:
• Convert
• Invert

Latin Root Word Meanings and Examples

---

20 Question

Latin Root: *fer*
Meaning: *to bring, or carry*
What words are examples for this root?

Latin Root Word Meanings and Examples

20 Answer

Examples:
• Transfer
• Inference

Latin Root Word Meanings and Examples

---

21 Question

Latin Root: *pos*
Meaning: *to place or put*
What words are examples for this root?

Latin Root Word Meanings and Examples

21 Answer

Examples:
• Deposit
• Preposition

Latin Root Word Meanings and Examples

---

22 Question

Latin Root: *struct*
Meaning: *to build*
What words are examples for this root?

Latin Root Word Meanings and Examples

22 Answer

Examples:
• Structure
• Reconstruct

Latin Root Word Meanings and Examples

---

23 Question

Latin Root: *vers*
Meaning: *to turn*
What words are examples for this root?

Latin Root Word Meanings and Examples

23 Answer

Examples:
• Aversion
• Subversive

Latin Root Word Meanings and Examples

---

24 Question

Latin Root: *ced*
Meaning: *go, lead, yield*
What words are examples for this root?

Latin Root Word Meanings and Examples

24 Answer

Examples:
• Intercede
• Recede

Latin Root Word Meanings and Examples

Latin Root
Word Meanings and Examples
(continued)

Directions: Copy enough cards so each student receives a card. Cut out the cards on the dotted line. Fold cards on solid line and tape or glue the Question and Answer card back to back.

25 *Question*
Latin Root: *frat*
Meaning: *brother*
What words are examples for this root?

Latin Root Word Meanings and Examples

25 *Answer*
Examples:
- Fraternal
- Fraternity

Latin Root Word Meanings and Examples

26 *Question*
Latin Root: *hab*
Meaning: *to have*
What words are examples for this root?

Latin Root Word Meanings and Examples

26 *Answer*
Examples:
- Inhabitant
- Rehabilitate

Latin Root Word Meanings and Examples

27 *Question*
Latin Root: *form*
Meaning: *shape*
What words are examples for this root?

Latin Root Word Meanings and Examples

27 *Answer*
Examples:
- Conform
- Formalize

Latin Root Word Meanings and Examples

28 *Question*
Latin Root: *turb*
Meaning: *turmoil*
What words are examples for this root?

Latin Root Word Meanings and Examples

28 *Answer*
Examples:
- Turbulent
- Disturb

Latin Root Word Meanings and Examples

29 *Question*
Latin Root: *fac*
Meaning: *to make or to do*
What words are examples for this root?

Latin Root Word Meanings and Examples

29 *Answer*
Examples:
- Factor
- Facile

Latin Root Word Meanings and Examples

30 *Question*
Latin Root: *part*
Meaning: *part*
What words are examples for this root?

Latin Root Word Meanings and Examples

30 *Answer*
Examples:
- Partial
- Partition

Latin Root Word Meanings and Examples

Latin Root
Word Meanings and Examples
(continued)

Directions: Copy enough cards so each student receives a card. Cut out the cards on the dotted line. Fold cards on solid line and tape or glue the Question and Answer card back to back.

31 Question
Latin Root: *son*
Meaning: *sound*
What words are examples for this root?
Latin Root Word Meanings and Examples

31 Answer
Examples:
• Resonate
• Consonant
Latin Root Word Meanings and Examples

32 Question
Latin Root: *dic*
Meaning: *to say or proclaim*
What words are examples for this root?
Latin Root Word Meanings and Examples

32 Answer
Examples:
• Abdicate
• Valedictorian
Latin Root Word Meanings and Examples

33 Question
Latin Root: *ces*
Meaning: *lead*
What words are examples for this root?
Latin Root Word Meanings and Examples

33 Answer
Examples:
• Access
• Incessant
Latin Root Word Meanings and Examples

34 Question
Latin Root: *plea*
Meaning: *to please*
What words are examples for this root?
Latin Root Word Meanings and Examples

34 Answer
Examples:
• Pleasantry
• Pleased
Latin Root Word Meanings and Examples

35 Question
Latin Root: *prim*
Meaning: *first*
What words are examples for this root?
Latin Root Word Meanings and Examples

35 Answer
Examples:
• Primitive
• Primeval
Latin Root Word Meanings and Examples

36 Question
Latin Root: *stit*
Meaning: *to stand*
What words are examples for this root?
Latin Root Word Meanings and Examples

36 Answer
Examples:
• Restitution
• Constituent
Latin Root Word Meanings and Examples

Latin Prefixes and Suffixes

Directions: Copy enough cards so each student receives a card. Cut out the cards on the dotted line. Fold cards on solid line and tape or glue the Question and Answer card back to back.

1 *Question*
Latin Prefix: *co*
What does it mean?
What word is an example?
Latin Prefixes and Suffixes

1 *Answer*
Meaning: together
Example: coexist
Latin Prefixes and Suffixes

2 *Question*
Latin Prefix: *de*
What does it mean?
What word is an example?
Latin Prefixes and Suffixes

2 *Answer*
Meaning: away or off
Example: decay
Latin Prefixes and Suffixes

3 *Question*
Latin Prefix: *dis*
What does it mean?
What word is an example?
Latin Prefixes and Suffixes

3 *Answer*
Meaning: not or not any
Example: disconnect
Latin Prefixes and Suffixes

4 *Question*
Latin Prefix: *inter*
What does it mean?
What word is an example?
Latin Prefixes and Suffixes

4 *Answer*
Meaning: between or among
Example: intervene
Latin Prefixes and Suffixes

5 *Question*
Latin Prefix: *non*
What does it mean?
What word is an example?
Latin Prefixes and Suffixes

5 *Answer*
Meaning: not
Example: nonentity
Latin Prefixes and Suffixes

6 *Question*
Latin Prefix: *post*
What does it mean?
What word is an example?
Latin Prefixes and Suffixes

6 *Answer*
Meaning: after
Example: postscript
Latin Prefixes and Suffixes

Latin Prefixes and Suffixes
(continued)

Directions: Copy enough cards so each student receives a card. Cut out the cards on the dotted line. Fold cards on solid line and tape or glue the Question and Answer card back to back.

7 *Question*

Latin Prefix: *pre*

What does it mean?
What word is an example?

Latin Prefixes and Suffixes

7 *Answer*

Meaning: before
Example: prelude

Latin Prefixes and Suffixes

8 *Question*

Latin Prefix: *re*

What does it mean?
What word is an example?

Latin Prefixes and Suffixes

8 *Answer*

Meaning: again, back
Example: rework

Latin Prefixes and Suffixes

9 *Question*

Latin Prefix: *sub*

What does it mean?
What word is an example?

Latin Prefixes and Suffixes

9 *Answer*

Meaning: under
Example: submerge

Latin Prefixes and Suffixes

10 *Question*

Latin Prefix: *trans*

What does it mean?
What word is an example?

Latin Prefixes and Suffixes

4 *Answer*

Meaning: across or beyond
Example: transcontinental

Latin Prefixes and Suffixes

11 *Question*

Latin Prefix: *in*

What does it mean?
What word is an example?

Latin Prefixes and Suffixes

11 *Answer*

Meaning: not, without
Example: indiscreet

Latin Prefixes and Suffixes

12 *Question*

Latin Prefix: *intra*

What does it mean?
What word is an example?

Latin Prefixes and Suffixes

12 *Answer*

Meaning: within
Example: intramural

Latin Prefixes and Suffixes

Latin Prefixes and Suffixes
(continued)

Directions: Copy enough cards so each student receives a card. Cut out the cards on the dotted line. Fold cards on solid line and tape or glue the Question and Answer card back to back.

13 Question
Latin Prefix: *super*
What does it mean?
What word is an example?
Latin Prefixes and Suffixes

13 Answer
Meaning: over, above, beyond
Example: superhuman
Latin Prefixes and Suffixes

14 Question
Latin Prefix: *ab*
What does it mean?
What word is an example?
Latin Prefixes and Suffixes

14 Answer
Meaning: away from
Example: abduction
Latin Prefixes and Suffixes

15 Question
Latin Prefix: *ex*
What does it mean?
What word is an example?
Latin Prefixes and Suffixes

15 Answer
Meaning: out of, beyond
Example: exhale
Latin Prefixes and Suffixes

16 Question
Latin Prefix: *extra*
What does it mean?
What word is an example?
Latin Prefixes and Suffixes

16 Answer
Meaning: beyond
Example: extraordinary
Latin Prefixes and Suffixes

17 Question
Latin Prefix: *contra*
What does it mean?
What word is an example?
Latin Prefixes and Suffixes

17 Answer
Meaning: against
Example: contradict
Latin Prefixes and Suffixes

18 Question
Latin Prefixes and Suffixes

18 Answer
Latin Prefixes and Suffixes

Latin Prefixes and Suffixes
(continued)

Directions: Copy enough cards so each student receives a card. Cut out the cards on the dotted line. Fold cards on solid line and tape or glue the Question and Answer card back to back.

19 *Question*

Latin Suffix: *ion*

What does it mean?
What word is an example?

Latin Prefixes and Suffixes

19 *Answer*

Meaning: being, result of
Example: isolation

Latin Prefixes and Suffixes

---

20 *Question*

Latin Suffix: *fy*

What does it mean?
What word is an example?

Latin Prefixes and Suffixes

20 *Answer*

Meaning: to make, do
Example: beautify

Latin Prefixes and Suffixes

---

21 *Question*

Latin Suffix: *ment*

What does it mean?
What word is an example?

Latin Prefixes and Suffixes

21 *Answer*

Meaning: a means or product
Example: statement

Latin Prefixes and Suffixes

---

22 *Question*

Latin Suffix: *ty*

What does it mean?
What word is an example?

Latin Prefixes and Suffixes

22 *Answer*

Meaning: the condition of or quality of
Example: society

Latin Prefixes and Suffixes

---

23 *Question*

Latin Suffix: *age*

What does it mean?
What word is an example?

Latin Prefixes and Suffixes

23 *Answer*

Meaning: belonging to something
Example: advantage

Latin Prefixes and Suffixes

---

24 *Question*

Latin Suffix: *ence*

What does it mean?
What word is an example?

Latin Prefixes and Suffixes

24 *Answer*

Meaning: state, fact or quality of
Example: excellence

Latin Prefixes and Suffixes

Latin Prefixes and Suffixes
(continued)

Directions: Copy enough cards so each student receives a card. Cut out the cards on the dotted line. Fold cards on solid line and tape or glue the Question and Answer card back to back.

25 Question
Latin Suffix: *ance*
What does it mean?
What word is an example?
Latin Prefixes and Suffixes

25 Answer
Meaning: a state of being
Example: fragrance
Latin Prefixes and Suffixes

26 Question
Latin Suffix: *al*
What does it mean?
What word is an example?
Latin Prefixes and Suffixes

26 Answer
Meaning: like or suitable for
Example: comical
Latin Prefixes and Suffixes

27 Question
Latin Suffix: *ous*
What does it mean?
What word is an example?
Latin Prefixes and Suffixes

27 Answer
Meaning: to be characterized by or having the quality of
Example: miscellaneous
Latin Prefixes and Suffixes

28 Question
Latin Suffix: *ly*
What does it mean?
What word is an example?
Latin Prefixes and Suffixes

28 Answer
Meaning: like or to the extent of
Example: softly
Latin Prefixes and Suffixes

29 Question
Latin Suffix: *ine*
What does it mean?
What word is an example?
Latin Prefixes and Suffixes

29 Answer
Meaning: nature of, similar to
Example: saccharine
Latin Prefixes and Suffixes

30 Question
Latin Suffix: *ate*
What does it mean?
What word is an example?
Latin Prefixes and Suffixes

30 Answer
Meaning: to become associated with
Example: collegiate
Latin Prefixes and Suffixes

Latin Prefixes and Suffixes
(continued)

Directions: Copy enough cards so each student receives a card. Cut out the cards on the dotted line. Fold cards on solid line and tape or glue the Question and Answer card back to back.

31 Question

Latin Suffix: *ible*

What does it mean?
What word is an example?

Latin Prefixes and Suffixes

31 Answer

Meaning: able or capable of being
Example: edible

Latin Prefixes and Suffixes

32 Question

Latin Suffix: *able*

What does it mean?
What word is an example?

Latin Prefixes and Suffixes

32 Answer

Meaning: capable of being
Example: portable

Latin Prefixes and Suffixes

33 Question

Latin Prefixes and Suffixes

33 Answer

Latin Prefixes and Suffixes

34 Question

Latin Prefixes and Suffixes

34 Answer

Latin Prefixes and Suffixes

35 Question

Latin Prefixes and Suffixes

35 Answer

Latin Prefixes and Suffixes

36 Question

Latin Prefixes and Suffixes

36 Answer

Latin Prefixes and Suffixes

Greek Root Word Meanings

Directions: Copy enough cards so each student receives a card. Cut out the cards on the dotted line. Fold cards on solid line and tape or glue the Question and Answer card back to back.

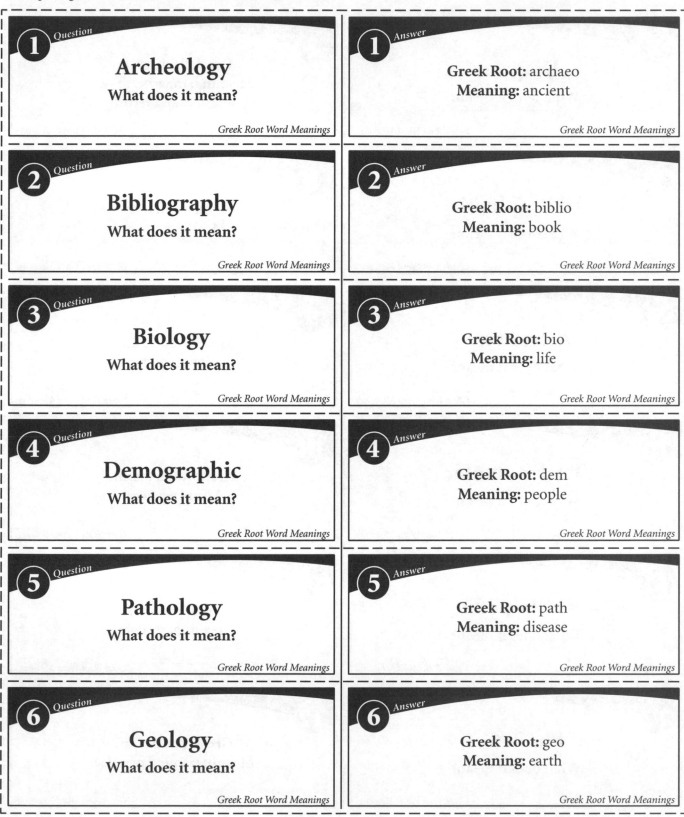

1 *Question*

Archeology

What does it mean?

Greek Root Word Meanings

1 *Answer*

Greek Root: archaeo
Meaning: ancient

Greek Root Word Meanings

2 *Question*

Bibliography

What does it mean?

Greek Root Word Meanings

2 *Answer*

Greek Root: biblio
Meaning: book

Greek Root Word Meanings

3 *Question*

Biology

What does it mean?

Greek Root Word Meanings

3 *Answer*

Greek Root: bio
Meaning: life

Greek Root Word Meanings

4 *Question*

Demographic

What does it mean?

Greek Root Word Meanings

4 *Answer*

Greek Root: dem
Meaning: people

Greek Root Word Meanings

5 *Question*

Pathology

What does it mean?

Greek Root Word Meanings

5 *Answer*

Greek Root: path
Meaning: disease

Greek Root Word Meanings

6 *Question*

Geology

What does it mean?

Greek Root Word Meanings

6 *Answer*

Greek Root: geo
Meaning: earth

Greek Root Word Meanings

Greek Root Word Meanings
(continued)

Directions: Copy enough cards so each student receives a card. Cut out the cards on the dotted line. Fold cards on solid line and tape or glue the Question and Answer card back to back.

7 Question

Diagram
What does it mean?

Greek Root Word Meanings

7 Answer

Greek Root: gram
Meaning: to write, draw, describe, and record

Greek Root Word Meanings

8 Question

Hydrophobia
What does it mean?

Greek Root Word Meanings

8 Answer

Greek Root: hydro
Meaning: water

Greek Root Word Meanings

9 Question

Astronomy
What does it mean?

Greek Root Word Meanings

9 Answer

Greek Root: astro
Meaning: star

Greek Root Word Meanings

10 Question

Thermometer
What does it mean?

Greek Root Word Meanings

10 Answer

Greek Root: therm
Meaning: heat

Greek Root Word Meanings

11 Question

Orthopedic
What does it mean?

Greek Root Word Meanings

11 Answer

Greek Root: orth
Meaning: straight

Greek Root Word Meanings

12 Question

Phonetics
What does it mean?

Greek Root Word Meanings

12 Answer

Greek Root: phon
Meaning: sound or voice

Greek Root Word Meanings

Greek Root Word Meanings

(continued)

Directions: Copy enough cards so each student receives a card. Cut out the cards on the dotted line. Fold cards on solid line and tape or glue the Question and Answer card back to back.

13 Question

Photosynthesis

What does it mean?

Greek Root Word Meanings

13 Answer

Greek Root: photo
Meaning: light

Greek Root Word Meanings

14 Question

Metropolis

What does it mean?

Greek Root Word Meanings

14 Answer

Greek Root: pol
Meaning: city

Greek Root Word Meanings

15 Question

Psychic

What does it mean?

Greek Root Word Meanings

15 Answer

Greek Root: psych
Meaning: mind, soul, or spirit

Greek Root Word Meanings

16 Question

Microscope

What does it mean?

Greek Root Word Meanings

16 Answer

Greek Root: scope
Meaning: to examine

Greek Root Word Meanings

17 Question

Automatic

What does it mean?

Greek Root Word Meanings

17 Answer

Greek Root: auto
Meaning: self

Greek Root Word Meanings

18 Question

Calligraphy

What does it mean?

Greek Root Word Meanings

18 Answer

Greek Root: calli
Meaning: beautiful

Greek Root Word Meanings

Greek Root Word Meanings
(continued)

Directions: Copy enough cards so each student receives a card. Cut out the cards on the dotted line. Fold cards on solid line and tape or glue the Question and Answer card back to back.

19 Question

Octagon
What does it mean?

Greek Root Word Meanings

19 Answer

Greek Root: oct
Meaning: eight

Greek Root Word Meanings

20 Question

Sympathy
What does it mean?

Greek Root Word Meanings

20 Answer

Greek Root: path
Meaning: feeling

Greek Root Word Meanings

21 Question

Zoology
What does it mean?

Greek Root Word Meanings

21 Answer

Greek Root: zo
Meaning: animal or living being

Greek Root Word Meanings

22 Question

Synchronize
What does it mean?

Greek Root Word Meanings

22 Answer

Greek Root: chron
Meaning: time

Greek Root Word Meanings

23 Question

Pediatrician
What does it mean?

Greek Root Word Meanings

23 Answer

Greek Root: ped
Meaning: child

Greek Root Word Meanings

24 Question

Seismograph
What does it mean?

Greek Root Word Meanings

24 Answer

Greek Root: sei
Meaning: shake

Greek Root Word Meanings

Greek Root Word Meanings
(continued)

Directions: Copy enough cards so each student receives a card. Cut out the cards on the dotted line. Fold cards on solid line and tape or glue the Question and Answer card back to back.

25 Question	**25** Answer
## Technology **What does it mean?** *Greek Root Word Meanings*	**Greek Root:** techno **Meaning:** art or skill *Greek Root Word Meanings*
26 Question	**26** Answer
## Physical **What does it mean?** *Greek Root Word Meanings*	**Greek Root:** physi **Meaning:** nature *Greek Root Word Meanings*
27 Question	**27** Answer
## Anthropology **What does it mean?** *Greek Root Word Meanings*	**Greek Root:** anthrop **Meaning:** man *Greek Root Word Meanings*
28 Question	**28** Answer
## Metamorphic **What does it mean?** *Greek Root Word Meanings*	**Greek Root:** morph **Meaning:** form *Greek Root Word Meanings*
29 Question	**29** Answer
## Synthesis **What does it mean?** *Greek Root Word Meanings*	**Greek Root:** syn **Meaning:** together *Greek Root Word Meanings*
30 Question	**30** Answer
## Cryptogram **What does it mean?** *Greek Root Word Meanings*	**Greek Root:** crypt **Meaning:** hidden *Greek Root Word Meanings*

Greek Prefixes and Suffixes

Directions: Copy enough cards so each student receives a card. Cut out the cards on the dotted line. Fold cards on solid line and tape or glue the Question and Answer card back to back.

1 *Question*

Greek Prefix: *anti*

What does it mean?
What word is an example?

Greek Prefixes and Suffixes

1 *Answer*

Meaning: against
Example: antibiotic

Greek Prefixes and Suffixes

2 *Question*

Greek Prefix: *auto*

What does it mean?
What word is an example?

Greek Prefixes and Suffixes

2 *Answer*

Meaning: self
Example: automatic

Greek Prefixes and Suffixes

3 *Question*

Greek Prefix: *deca/dec*

What does it mean?
What word is an example?

Greek Prefixes and Suffixes

3 *Answer*

Meaning: ten
Example: decade

Greek Prefixes and Suffixes

4 *Question*

Greek Prefix: *dia*

What does it mean?
What word is an example?

Greek Prefixes and Suffixes

4 *Answer*

Meaning: across
Example: diameter

Greek Prefixes and Suffixes

5 *Question*

Greek Prefix: *dys*

What does it mean?
What word is an example?

Greek Prefixes and Suffixes

5 *Answer*

Meaning: difficult, bad
Example: dysfunctional

Greek Prefixes and Suffixes

6 *Question*

Greek Prefix: *hemi*

What does it mean?
What word is an example?

Greek Prefixes and Suffixes

6 *Answer*

Meaning: half
Example: hemisphere

Greek Prefixes and Suffixes

Greek Prefixes and Suffixes
(continued)

Directions: Copy enough cards so each student receives a card. Cut out the cards on the dotted line. Fold cards on solid line and tape or glue the Question and Answer card back to back.

 7 Question

Greek Prefix: *bot*

What does it mean?
What word is an example?

Greek Prefixes and Suffixes

 7 Answer

Meaning: plant
Example: botany

Greek Prefixes and Suffixes

 8 Question

Greek Prefix: *baro*

What does it mean?
What word is an example?

Greek Prefixes and Suffixes

 8 Answer

Meaning: weight or pressure
Example: barometer

Greek Prefixes and Suffixes

 9 Question

Greek Prefix: *meg*

What does it mean?
What word is an example?

Greek Prefixes and Suffixes

 9 Answer

Meaning: great or large
Example: megaton

Greek Prefixes and Suffixes

 10 Question

Greek Prefix: *micro*

What does it mean?
What word is an example?

Greek Prefixes and Suffixes

 10 Answer

Meaning: small
Example: microchip

Greek Prefixes and Suffixes

 11 Question

Greek Prefix: *mono*

What does it mean?
What word is an example?

Greek Prefixes and Suffixes

 11 Answer

Meaning: one, single
Example: monologue

Greek Prefixes and Suffixes

 12 Question

Greek Prefix: *neo*

What does it mean?
What word is an example?

Greek Prefixes and Suffixes

 12 Answer

Meaning: new
Example: neonatal

Greek Prefixes and Suffixes

Greek Prefixes and Suffixes
(continued)

Directions: Copy enough cards so each student receives a card. Cut out the cards on the dotted line. Fold cards on solid line and tape or glue the Question and Answer card back to back.

---

13 Question

Greek Prefix: *paleo*

What does it mean?
What word is an example?

Greek Prefixes and Suffixes

13 Answer

Meaning: long ago, ancient
Example: paleontologist

Greek Prefixes and Suffixes

---

14 Question

Greek Prefix: *peri*

What does it mean?
What word is an example?

Greek Prefixes and Suffixes

14 Answer

Meaning: around, about
Example: perimeter

Greek Prefixes and Suffixes

---

15 Question

Greek Prefix: *poly*

What does it mean?
What word is an example?

Greek Prefixes and Suffixes

15 Answer

Meaning: many
Example: polygon

Greek Prefixes and Suffixes

---

16 Question

Greek Prefix: *pseudo*

What does it mean?
What word is an example?

Greek Prefixes and Suffixes

16 Answer

Meaning: false, counterfeit
Example: pseudonym

Greek Prefixes and Suffixes

---

17 Question

Greek Prefix: *super/supra*

What does it mean?
What word is an example?

Greek Prefixes and Suffixes

17 Answer

Meaning: above or beyond
Example: supernova

Greek Prefixes and Suffixes

---

18 Question

Greek Prefix: *syn/sym*

What does it mean?
What word is an example?

Greek Prefixes and Suffixes

18 Answer

Meaning: together, with
Example: synchronize and sympathy

Greek Prefixes and Suffixes

Greek Prefixes and Suffixes
(continued)

Directions: Copy enough cards so each student receives a card. Cut out the cards on the dotted line. Fold cards on solid line and tape or glue the Question and Answer card back to back.

19 *Question*

Greek Suffix: *ist*

What does it mean?
What word is an example?

Greek Prefixes and Suffixes

19 *Answer*

Meaning: one who
practices or is a follower
Example: conformist

Greek Prefixes and Suffixes

20 *Question*

Greek Suffix: *ism*

What does it mean?
What word is an example?

Greek Prefixes and Suffixes

20 *Answer*

Meaning: the belief or practice of
Example: capitalism

Greek Prefixes and Suffixes

21 *Question*

Greek Suffix: *ome*

What does it mean?
What word is an example?

Greek Prefixes and Suffixes

21 *Answer*

Meaning: a body or
large group of something
Example: biome

Greek Prefixes and Suffixes

22 *Question*

Greek Suffix: *oid*

What does it mean?
What word is an example?

Greek Prefixes and Suffixes

22 *Answer*

Meaning: resembling,
like, or shaped like something
Example: asteroid

Greek Prefixes and Suffixes

23 *Question*

Greek Suffix: *sis*

What does it mean?
What word is an example?

Greek Prefixes and Suffixes

23 *Answer*

Meaning: act, state, or condition of
Example: analysis

Greek Prefixes and Suffixes

24 *Question*

Greek Suffix: *isk*

What does it mean?
What word is an example?

Greek Prefixes and Suffixes

24 *Answer*

Meaning: small
Example: asterisk

Greek Prefixes and Suffixes

Greek Prefixes and Suffixes
(continued)

Directions: Copy enough cards so each student receives a card. Cut out the cards on the dotted line. Fold cards on solid line and tape or glue the Question and Answer card back to back.

25 Question
Greek Suffix: *ical*
What does it mean?
What word is an example?
Greek Prefixes and Suffixes

25 Answer
Meaning: pertaining to
Example: electrical
Greek Prefixes and Suffixes

26 Question
Greek Suffix: *logue*
What does it mean?
What word is an example?
Greek Prefixes and Suffixes

26 Answer
Meaning: to speak
Example: dialogue
Greek Prefixes and Suffixes

27 Question
Greek Suffix: *logy*
What does it mean?
What word is an example?
Greek Prefixes and Suffixes

27 Answer
Meaning: discourse or theory
Example: biology
Greek Prefixes and Suffixes

28 Question
Greek Suffix: *phobia*
What does it mean?
What word is an example?
Greek Prefixes and Suffixes

28 Answer
Meaning: an intense fear of a specific thing
Example: hydrophobia
Greek Prefixes and Suffixes

29 Question
Greek Suffix: *phone*
What does it mean?
What word is an example?
Greek Prefixes and Suffixes

29 Answer
Meaning: a device that receives sound or speaker of a language
Example: homophone or telephone
Greek Prefixes and Suffixes

30 Question
Greek Suffix: *meter*
What does it mean?
What word is an example?
Greek Prefixes and Suffixes

30 Answer
Meaning: measuring device
Example: kilometer
Greek Prefixes and Suffixes

Elements of a Short Story

Directions: Copy enough cards so each student receives a card. Cut out the cards on the dotted line. Fold cards on solid line and tape or glue the Question and Answer card back to back.

---

1 Question

What is the role of the *antagonist* in a story?

Elements of a Short Story

1 Answer

The *antagonist* is the force opposing the protagonist. The *antagonist* is usually the bad guy.

Elements of a Short Story

---

2 Question

What is an *autobiography*?

Elements of a Short Story

2 Answer

An *autobiography* is the true story of someone's life told in first person.

Elements of a Short Story

---

3 Question

Where is the *climax* in a story?

Elements of a Short Story

3 Answer

The *climax* is the high point in the story where conflict is resolved.

Elements of a Short Story

---

4 Question

What creates *conflict* in a story?

Elements of a Short Story

4 Answer

The opposing force(s) between the protagonist and antagonist create the *conflict*.

Elements of a Short Story

---

5 Question

What is the role of *exposition* in a story?

Elements of a Short Story

5 Answer

Exposition is the background information for the story.

Elements of a Short Story

---

6 Question

What brings about the *falling action* in a story?

Elements of a Short Story

6 Answer

Falling action is a series of actions bringing the story to its end.

Elements of a Short Story

Elements of a Short Story (continued)

Directions: Copy enough cards so each student receives a card. Cut out the cards on the dotted line. Fold cards on solid line and tape or glue the Question and Answer card back to back.

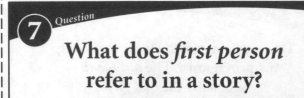

7 Question

What does *first person* refer to in a story?

Elements of a Short Story

7 Answer

First person is telling the story from the "I" point of view.

Elements of a Short Story

8 Question

Who is a *flat character*?

Elements of a Short Story

8 Answer

A *flat character* is one who appears as a stereotype in the story.

Elements of a Short Story

9 Question

What is *plot*?

Elements of a Short Story

9 Answer

Plot is the events that outline the story.

Elements of a Short Story

10 Question

What is *point of view*?

Elements of a Short Story

10 Answer

Point of view is the position from which the story is told to the reader.

Elements of a Short Story

11 Question

What is the role of the *protagonist* in a story?

Elements of a Short Story

11 Answer

The *protagonist* is the hero or heroine of the story.

Elements of a Short Story

12 Question

What is *resolution*?

Elements of a Short Story

12 Answer

Resolution is the ending of the story plot, or how it turns out.

Elements of a Short Story

Elements of a Short Story (continued)

Directions: Copy enough cards so each student receives a card. Cut out the cards on the dotted line. Fold cards on solid line and tape or glue the Question and Answer card back to back.

---

13 Question

What is the *rising action* in a story?

Elements of a Short Story

13 Answer

Rising action is the story plot that builds to the climax.

Elements of a Short Story

---

14 Question

Who is the *rounded character*?

Elements of a Short Story

14 Answer

The *rounded character* is one who comes across as an authentic person.

Elements of a Short Story

---

15 Question

What is *setting*?

Elements of a Short Story

15 Answer

Setting is where the story takes place.

Elements of a Short Story

---

16 Question

What is a *short story*?

Elements of a Short Story

16 Answer

A *short story* is a work of prose that can be read in one sitting.

Elements of a Short Story

---

17 Question

What is *theme*?

Elements of a Short Story

17 Answer

Theme is the main idea or message of the story.

Elements of a Short Story

---

18 Question

What does *third person* refer to in a story?

Elements of a Short Story

18 Answer

The *third person* is the story being told from the "he/she/they" point of view.

Elements of a Short Story

Elements of a Short Story *(continued)*

Directions: Copy enough cards so each student receives a card. Cut out the cards on the dotted line. Fold cards on solid line and tape or glue the Question and Answer card back to back.

19 Question **What is *tone*?** *Elements of a Short Story*	**19** Answer *Tone* is the author's attitude toward his or her subject. *Elements of a Short Story*
20 Question *Elements of a Short Story*	**20** Answer *Elements of a Short Story*
21 Question *Elements of a Short Story*	**21** Answer *Elements of a Short Story*
22 Question *Elements of a Short Story*	**22** Answer *Elements of a Short Story*
23 Question *Elements of a Short Story*	**23** Answer *Elements of a Short Story*
24 Question *Elements of a Short Story*	**24** Answer *Elements of a Short Story*

Text Types—Definitions

Directions: Copy enough cards so each student receives a card. Cut out the cards on the dotted line. Fold cards on solid line and tape or glue the Question and Answer card back to back.

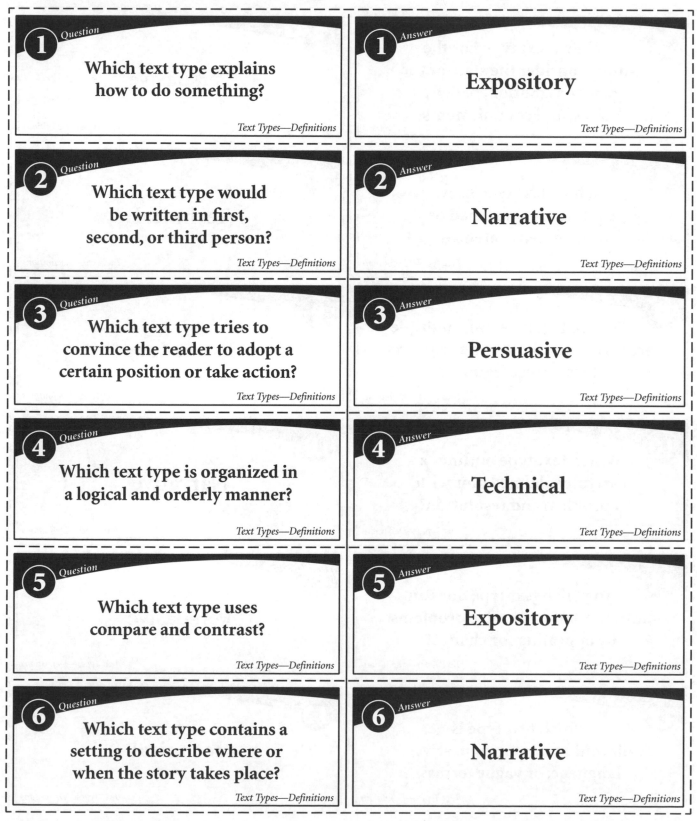

1 Question

Which text type explains
how to do something?

Text Types—Definitions

1 Answer

Expository

Text Types—Definitions

2 Question

Which text type would
be written in first,
second, or third person?

Text Types—Definitions

2 Answer

Narrative

Text Types—Definitions

3 Question

Which text type tries to
convince the reader to adopt a
certain position or take action?

Text Types—Definitions

3 Answer

Persuasive

Text Types—Definitions

4 Question

Which text type is organized in
a logical and orderly manner?

Text Types—Definitions

4 Answer

Technical

Text Types—Definitions

5 Question

Which text type uses
compare and contrast?

Text Types—Definitions

5 Answer

Expository

Text Types—Definitions

6 Question

Which text type contains a
setting to describe where or
when the story takes place?

Text Types—Definitions

6 Answer

Narrative

Text Types—Definitions

Text Types—Definitions (continued)

Directions: Copy enough cards so each student receives a card. Cut out the cards on the dotted line. Fold cards on solid line and tape or glue the Question and Answer card back to back.

7 Question
Which text type has the author consider the state of the reader's emotion, beliefs, desires, and commitments?
Text Types—Definitions

7 Answer
Persuasive
Text Types—Definitions

8 Question
Which text type uses commonly shortened or fragmented sentences?
Text Types—Definitions

8 Answer
Technical
Text Types—Definitions

9 Question
Which text type uses multiple organizational patterns as context clues or text features?
Text Types—Definitions

9 Answer
Expository
Text Types—Definitions

10 Question
Which text type outlines a carefully planned plot with a problem and resolution?
Text Types—Definitions

10 Answer
Narrative
Text Types—Definitions

11 Question
In which text type does an author attempt to solve problems by appealing for change?
Text Types—Definitions

11 Answer
Persuasive
Text Types—Definitions

12 Question
Which text type is devoid of humor, figurative language, or vague terms?
Text Types—Definitions

12 Answer
Technical
Text Types—Definitions

Text Types—Definitions (continued)

Directions: Copy enough cards so each student receives a card. Cut out the cards on the dotted line. Fold cards on solid line and tape or glue the Question and Answer card back to back.

13 Question
Which text type uses patterns signaled by different headings, subheadings, and signal words?
Text Types—Definitions

13 Answer
Expository
Text Types—Definitions

14 Question
Which text type contains a theme that explains the meaning behind the story?
Text Types—Definitions

14 Answer
Narrative
Text Types—Definitions

15 Question
Which text type uses testimonials, statistics, or the bandwagon approach to prove its points?
Text Types—Definitions

15 Answer
Persuasive
Text Types—Definitions

16 Question
Which text type focuses on an identified topic using numbered or bulleted lists?
Text Types—Definitions

16 Answer
Technical
Text Types—Definitions

17 Question
Which text type is difficult to predict based on its content?
Text Types—Definitions

17 Answer
Expository
Text Types—Definitions

18 Question
Which text type contains vocabulary used to enrich the understanding of the story?
Text Types—Definitions

18 Answer
Narrative
Text Types—Definitions

Text Types—Definitions (continued)

Directions: Copy enough cards so each student receives a card. Cut out the cards on the dotted line. Fold cards on solid line and tape or glue the Question and Answer card back to back.

19 Question

Which text type takes a stand on an issue?

Text Types—Definitions

19 Answer

Persuasive

Text Types—Definitions

20 Question

Which text type uses domain-specific terminology?

Text Types—Definitions

20 Answer

Technical

Text Types—Definitions

21 Question

Which text type presents facts and information based on clear and precise dialogue?

Text Types—Definitions

21 Answer

Expository

Text Types—Definitions

22 Question

Which text type tells a story using well-developed characters?

Text Types—Definitions

22 Answer

Narrative

Text Types—Definitions

23 Question

Which text type focuses on a central purpose and sometimes relies on propaganda and sarcasm?

Text Types—Definitions

23 Answer

Persuasive

Text Types—Definitions

24 Question

Which text type has a hierarchical organization where information may bc acccssed at random?

Text Types—Definitions

24 Answer

Technical

Text Types—Definitions

Text Types—Definitions (continued)

Directions: Copy enough cards so each student receives a card. Cut out the cards on the dotted line. Fold cards on solid line and tape or glue the Question and Answer card back to back.

25 Question
Which text type is used to describe a problem and its solution?
Text Types—Definitions

25 Answer
Expository
Text Types—Definitions

26 Question
Which text type helps the reader determine and explain the theme of a story?
Text Types—Definitions

26 Answer
Narrative
Text Types—Definitions

27 Question
Which text type demonstrates the author using reasoning to prove a point?
Text Types—Definitions

27 Answer
Persuasive
Text Types—Definitions

28 Question
Which text type relies on the dictionary meaning of words?
Text Types—Definitions

28 Answer
Technical
Text Types—Definitions

29 Question
Which text type suggests cause and effect in its text?
Text Types—Definitions

29 Answer
Technical
Text Types—Definitions

30 Question
Which text type uses text features to convey information?
Text Types—Definitions

30 Answer
Expository
Text Types—Definitions

Text Types—Structures

Directions: Copy enough cards so each student receives a card. Cut out the cards on the dotted line. Fold cards on solid line and tape or glue the Question and Answer card back to back.

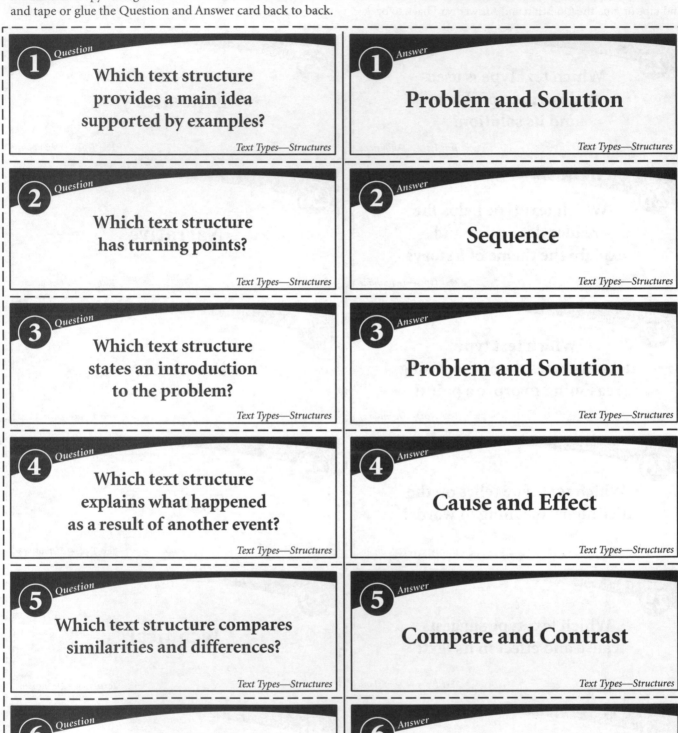

1 Question
Which text structure provides a main idea supported by examples?

Text Types—Structures

1 Answer
Problem and Solution

Text Types—Structures

2 Question
Which text structure has turning points?

Text Types—Structures

2 Answer
Sequence

Text Types—Structures

3 Question
Which text structure states an introduction to the problem?

Text Types—Structures

3 Answer
Problem and Solution

Text Types—Structures

4 Question
Which text structure explains what happened as a result of another event?

Text Types—Structures

4 Answer
Cause and Effect

Text Types—Structures

5 Question
Which text structure compares similarities and differences?

Text Types—Structures

5 Answer
Compare and Contrast

Text Types—Structures

6 Question
Which text structure attempts to bring resolution to an issue?

Text Types—Structures

6 Answer
Problem and Solution

Text Types—Structures

Text Types—Structures (continued)

Directions: Copy enough cards so each student receives a card. Cut out the cards on the dotted line. Fold cards on solid line and tape or glue the Question and Answer card back to back.

7 *Question*
Which text structure uses the words *additionally* and *another*?

Text Types—Structures

7 *Answer*
Sequence

Text Types—Structures

8 *Question*
Which text structure uses "for example" as a key term?

Text Types—Structures

8 *Answer*
Description

Text Types—Structures

9 *Question*
Which text structure explains reasons why or how something happens?

Text Types—Structures

9 *Answer*
Cause and Effect

Text Types—Structures

10 *Question*
Which text structure has a main idea with supporting details?

Text Types—Structures

10 *Answer*
Description

Text Types—Structures

11 *Question*
Which text structure puts facts, events, or concepts in order of their occurrence?

Text Types—Structures

11 *Answer*
Sequence

Text Types—Structures

12 *Question*
Which text structure lists pieces of information?

Text Types—Structures

12 *Answer*
Description

Text Types—Structures

Text Types—Structures (continued)

Directions: Copy enough cards so each student receives a card. Cut out the cards on the dotted line. Fold cards on solid line and tape or glue the Question and Answer card back to back.

---

13 Question

Which text structure describes an influence and the effect it had on you?

Text Types—Structures

13 Answer

Cause and Effect

Text Types—Structures

---

14 Question

Which text structure follows step by step through time, place, person, or thing?

Text Types—Structures

14 Answer

Description

Text Types—Structures

---

15 Question

Which text structure presents information point by point?

Text Types—Structures

15 Answer

Compare and Contrast

Text Types—Structures

---

16 Question

Which text structure uses the signal words *most important, for instance*?

Text Types—Structures

16 Answer

Description

Text Types—Structures

---

17 Question

Which text structure uses the signal words *not long after, first, finally*?

Text Types—Structures

17 Answer

Sequence

Text Types—Structures

---

18 Question

Which text structure uses the signal words *because, consequently, this led to*?

Text Types—Structures

18 Answer

Cause and Effect

Text Types—Structures

Text Types—Structures (continued)

Directions: Copy enough cards so each student receives a card. Cut out the cards on the dotted line. Fold cards on solid line and tape or glue the Question and Answer card back to back.

19 *Question*
Which text structure uses the signal words *therefore, as a result, so that*?
Text Types—Structures

19 *Answer*
Problem and Solution
Text Types—Structures

20 *Question*
Which text structure uses the signal words *however, on the other hand, compared to*?
Text Types—Structures

20 *Answer*
Compare and Contrast
Text Types—Structures

21 *Question*
Which text structure is used when writing a personal story?
Text Types—Structures

21 *Answer*
Narrative
Text Types—Structures

22 *Question*
Which text structure may be used in research writing?
Text Types—Structures

22 *Answer*
Expository
Text Types—Structures

23 *Question*
Which text structure proposes a remedy to a problem?
Text Types—Structures

23 *Answer*
Problem and Solution
Text Types—Structures

24 *Question*
Which text structure explains the likenesses and differences among facts, events, or people?
Text Types—Structures

24 *Answer*
Compare and Contrast
Text Types—Structures

Text Types—Structures (continued)

Directions: Copy enough cards so each student receives a card. Cut out the cards on the dotted line. Fold cards on solid line and tape or glue the Question and Answer card back to back.

25 Question **Which text structure shows how facts or events happen because of other facts or events?** *Text Types—Structures*	**25** Answer **Cause and Effect** *Text Types—Structures*
26 Question **Which text structure uses analysis to demonstrate a point?** *Text Types—Structures*	**26** Answer **Compare and Contrast** *Text Types—Structures*
27 Question **Which text structure focuses on character development?** *Text Types—Structures*	**27** Answer **Description** *Text Types—Structures*
28 Question **Which text structure attempts to convince the reader of the need for change and its solution?** *Text Types—Structures*	**28** Answer **Problem and Solution** *Text Types—Structures*
29 Question **Which text structure follows an orderly accounting of information?** *Text Types—Structures*	**29** Answer **Sequence** *Text Types—Structures*
30 Question **Which text structure provides a reason for the relationship of issues?** *Text Types—Structures*	**30** Answer **Cause and Effect** *Text Types—Structures*

Text Types—Examples

Directions: Copy enough cards so each student receives a card. Cut out the cards on the dotted line. Fold cards on solid line and tape or glue the Question and Answer card back to back.

1 Question

Brochures are an example of which text type?

Text Types—Examples

1 Answer

Expository

Text Types—Examples

2 Question

Historical fiction is an example of which text type?

Text Types—Examples

2 Answer

Narrative

Text Types—Examples

3 Question

Editorials are an example of which text type?

Text Types—Examples

3 Answer

Persuasive

Text Types—Examples

4 Question

Graphs and charts are an example of which text type?

Text Types—Examples

4 Answer

Technical

Text Types—Examples

5 Question

Autobiographies and biographies can both be an example of which text type?

Text Types—Examples

5 Answer

Expository

Text Types—Examples

6 Question

Legends and myths are an example of which text type?

Text Types—Examples

6 Answer

Narrative

Text Types—Examples

Text Types—Examples (continued)

Directions: Copy enough cards so each student receives a card. Cut out the cards on the dotted line. Fold cards on solid line and tape or glue the Question and Answer card back to back.

7 Question

Book reviews and movie critiques are an example of which text type?

Text Types—Examples

7 Answer

Persuasive

Text Types—Examples

8 Question

Instructions and how-to guides are an example of which text type?

Text Types—Examples

8 Answer

Technical

Text Types—Examples

9 Question

Research papers and speeches are an example of which text type?

Text Types—Examples

9 Answer

Expository

Text Types—Examples

10 Question

A drama or play is an example of which text type?

Text Types—Examples

10 Answer

Narrative

Text Types—Examples

11 Question

Campaign literature is an example of which text type?

Text Types—Examples

11 Answer

Persuasive

Text Types—Examples

12 Question

Documented regulations are an example of which text type?

Text Types—Examples

12 Answer

Technical

Text Types—Examples

Text Types—Examples *(continued)*

Directions: Copy enough cards so each student receives a card. Cut out the cards on the dotted line. Fold cards on solid line and tape or glue the Question and Answer card back to back.

13 Question

A book report is an example of which text type?

Text Types—Examples

13 Answer

Expository

Text Types—Examples

14 Question

Poetry is an example of which text type?

Text Types—Examples

14 Answer

Narrative

Text Types—Examples

15 Question

Posters advertising products are an example of which text type?

Text Types—Examples

15 Answer

Persuasive

Text Types—Examples

16 Question

Job preparation manuals are an example of which text type?

Text Types—Examples

16 Answer

Technical

Text Types—Examples

17 Question

Newspaper and magazine articles are an example of which text type?

Text Types—Examples

17 Answer

Expository

Text Types—Examples

18 Question

A personal narrative is an example of which text type?

Text Types—Examples

18 Answer

Narrative

Text Types—Examples

Text Types—Examples (continued)

Directions: Copy enough cards so each student receives a card. Cut out the cards on the dotted line. Fold cards on solid line and tape or glue the Question and Answer card back to back.

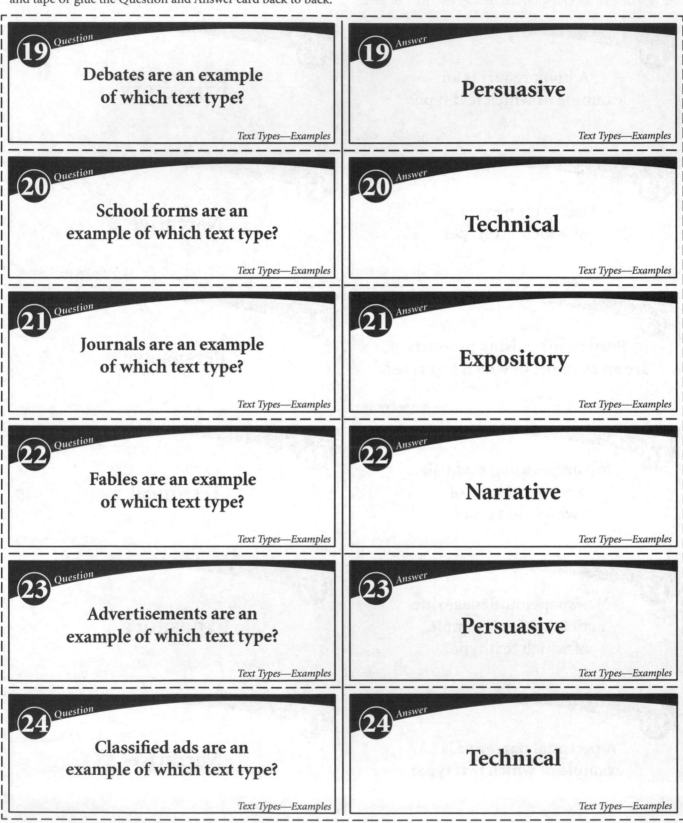

19 Question

Debates are an example
of which text type?

Text Types—Examples

19 Answer

Persuasive

Text Types—Examples

20 Question

School forms are an
example of which text type?

Text Types—Examples

20 Answer

Technical

Text Types—Examples

21 Question

Journals are an example
of which text type?

Text Types—Examples

21 Answer

Expository

Text Types—Examples

22 Question

Fables are an example
of which text type?

Text Types—Examples

22 Answer

Narrative

Text Types—Examples

23 Question

Advertisements are an
example of which text type?

Text Types—Examples

23 Answer

Persuasive

Text Types—Examples

24 Question

Classified ads are an
example of which text type?

Text Types—Examples

24 Answer

Technical

Text Types—Examples

Text Types—Examples (continued)

Directions: Copy enough cards so each student receives a card. Cut out the cards on the dotted line. Fold cards on solid line and tape or glue the Question and Answer card back to back.

25 Question Essays are an example of which text type? *Text Types—Examples*	**25** Answer **Expository** *Text Types—Examples*
26 Question Short stories are an example of which text type? *Text Types—Examples*	**26** Answer **Narrative** *Text Types—Examples*
27 Question Commercials are an example of which text type? *Text Types—Examples*	**27** Answer **Persuasive** *Text Types—Examples*
28 Question Recipes are an example of which text type? *Text Types—Examples*	**28** Answer **Technical** *Text Types—Examples*
29 Question Interviews are an example of which text type? *Text Types—Examples*	**29** Answer **Expository** *Text Types—Examples*
30 Question Science fiction is an example of which text type? *Text Types—Examples*	**30** Answer **Narrative** *Text Types—Examples*

Text Types—Structures
with Graphic Organizers

Directions: Copy enough cards so each student receives a card. Cut out the cards on the dotted line. Fold cards on solid line and tape or glue the Question and Answer card back to back.

1 Question
Which text structure would use this graphic organizer?

Text Types—Structures with Graphic Organizers

1 Answer

Compare and Contrast

Text Types—Structures with Graphic Organizers

2 Question
Which text structure would use this graphic organizer?

Text Types—Structures with Graphic Organizers

2 Answer

Problem and Solution

Text Types—Structures with Graphic Organizers

3 Question
Which text structure would use this graphic organizer?

Text Types—Structures with Graphic Organizers

3 Answer

Cause and Effect

Text Types—Structures with Graphic Organizers

Text Types—Structures with Graphic Organizers (continued)

Directions: Copy enough cards so each student receives a card. Cut out the cards on the dotted line. Fold cards on solid line and tape or glue the Question and Answer card back to back.

4 Question
Which text structure would use this graphic organizer?

Text Types—Structures with Graphic Organizers

4 Answer

Cause and Effect

Text Types—Structures with Graphic Organizers

5 Question
Which text structure would use this graphic organizer?

K	W	L

Text Types—Structures with Graphic Organizers

5 Answer

Description

Text Types—Structures with Graphic Organizers

6 Question
Which text structure would use this graphic organizer?

Title

Text Types—Structures with Graphic Organizers

6 Answer

Sequence

Text Types—Structures with Graphic Organizers

Text Types—Structures with Graphic Organizers *(continued)*

Directions: Copy enough cards so each student receives a card. Cut out the cards on the dotted line. Fold cards on solid line and tape or glue the Question and Answer card back to back.

7 Question
Which text structure would use this graphic organizer?

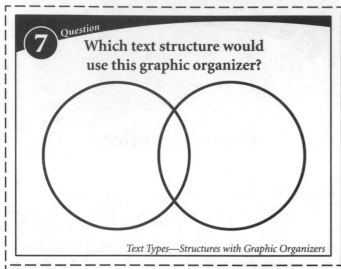

Text Types—Structures with Graphic Organizers

7 Answer

Compare and Contrast

Text Types—Structures with Graphic Organizers

8 Question
Which text structure would use this graphic organizer?

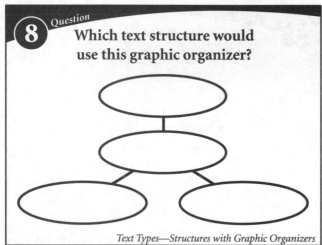

Text Types—Structures with Graphic Organizers

8 Answer

Description

Text Types—Structures with Graphic Organizers

9 Question
Which text structure would use this graphic organizer?

1. _____
2. _____
3. _____
4. _____
5. _____

Text Types—Structures with Graphic Organizers

9 Answer

Sequence

Text Types—Structures with Graphic Organizers

Text Types—Structures
with Graphic Organizers *(continued)*

Directions: Copy enough cards so each student receives a card. Cut out the cards on the dotted line. Fold cards on solid line and tape or glue the Question and Answer card back to back.

10 *Question*
Which text structure would use this graphic organizer?

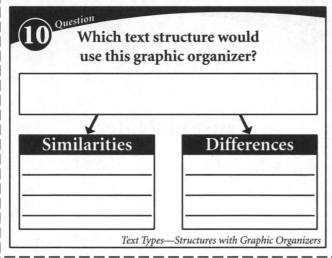

Text Types—Structures with Graphic Organizers

10 *Answer*

Compare and Contrast

Text Types—Structures with Graphic Organizers

11 *Question*
Which text structure would use this graphic organizer?

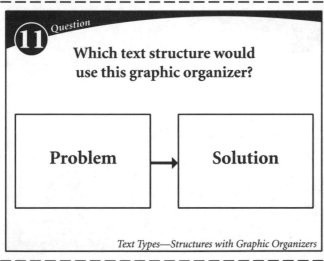

Text Types—Structures with Graphic Organizers

11 *Answer*

Problem and Solution

Text Types—Structures with Graphic Organizers

12 *Question*
Which text structure would use this graphic organizer?

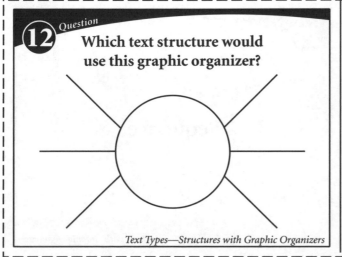

Text Types—Structures with Graphic Organizers

12 *Answer*

Description

Text Types—Structures with Graphic Organizers

Text Types—Structures
with Graphic Organizers (continued)

Directions: Copy enough cards so each student receives a card. Cut out the cards on the dotted line. Fold cards on solid line and tape or glue the Question and Answer card back to back.

13 Question
Which text structure would use this graphic organizer?

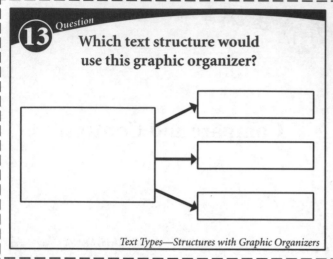

Text Types—Structures with Graphic Organizers

13 Answer

Cause and Effect

Text Types—Structures with Graphic Organizers

14 Question
Which text structure would use this graphic organizer?

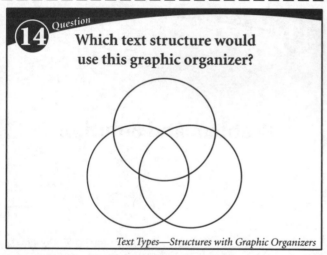

Text Types—Structures with Graphic Organizers

14 Answer

Compare and Contrast

Text Types—Structures with Graphic Organizers

15 Question
Which text structure would use this graphic organizer?

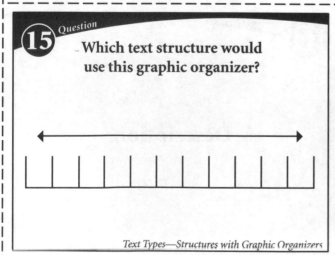

Text Types—Structures with Graphic Organizers

15 Answer

Sequence

Text Types—Structures with Graphic Organizers

Text Types—Structures with Graphic Organizers *(continued)*

Directions: Copy enough cards so each student receives a card. Cut out the cards on the dotted line. Fold cards on solid line and tape or glue the Question and Answer card back to back.

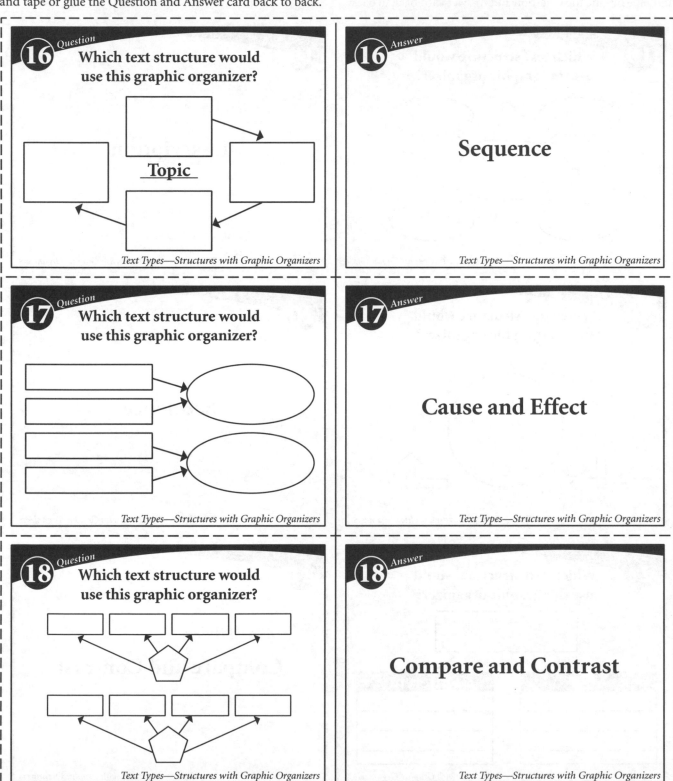

16 *Question*
Which text structure would use this graphic organizer?

Topic

Text Types—Structures with Graphic Organizers

16 *Answer*

Sequence

Text Types—Structures with Graphic Organizers

17 *Question*
Which text structure would use this graphic organizer?

Text Types—Structures with Graphic Organizers

17 *Answer*

Cause and Effect

Text Types—Structures with Graphic Organizers

18 *Question*
Which text structure would use this graphic organizer?

Text Types—Structures with Graphic Organizers

18 *Answer*

Compare and Contrast

Text Types—Structures with Graphic Organizers

Text Types—Structures with Graphic Organizers *(continued)*

Directions: Copy enough cards so each student receives a card. Cut out the cards on the dotted line. Fold cards on solid line and tape or glue the Question and Answer card back to back.

19 Question
Which text structure would use this graphic organizer?

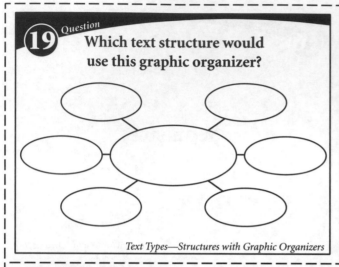

Text Types—Structures with Graphic Organizers

19 Answer

Description

Text Types—Structures with Graphic Organizers

20 Question
Which text structure would use this graphic organizer?

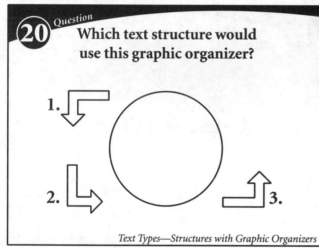

Text Types—Structures with Graphic Organizers

20 Answer

Sequence

Text Types—Structures with Graphic Organizers

21 Question
Which text structure would use this graphic organizer?

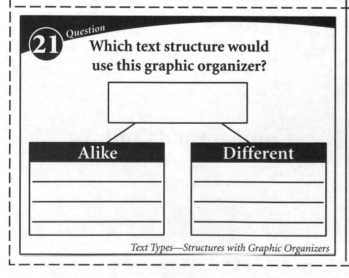

Alike   Different

Text Types—Structures with Graphic Organizers

21 Answer

Compare and Contrast

Text Types—Structures with Graphic Organizers

Text Types—Structures with Graphic Organizers *(continued)*

Directions: Copy enough cards so each student receives a card. Cut out the cards on the dotted line. Fold cards on solid line and tape or glue the Question and Answer card back to back.

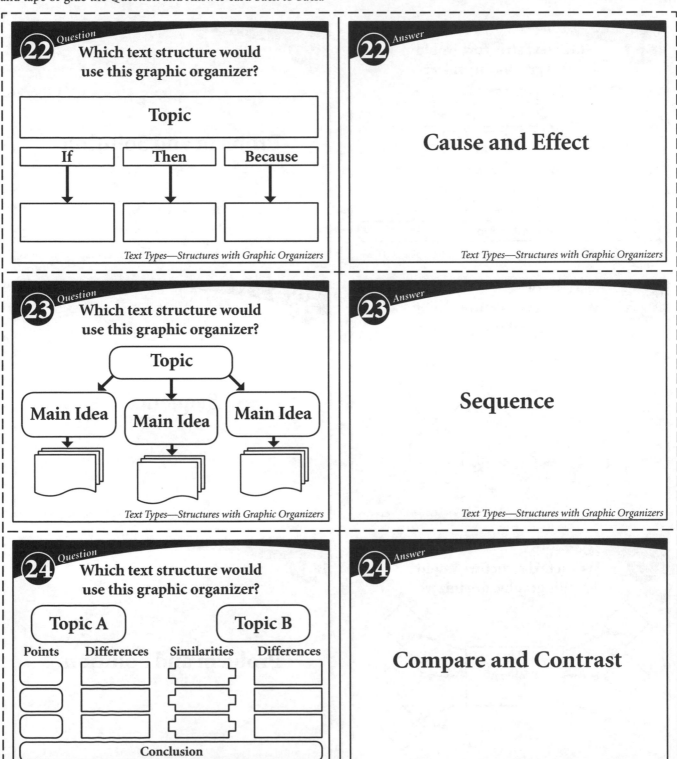

22 *Question*
Which text structure would use this graphic organizer?

Topic		
If	Then	Because

Text Types—Structures with Graphic Organizers

22 *Answer*

Cause and Effect

Text Types—Structures with Graphic Organizers

23 *Question*
Which text structure would use this graphic organizer?

Topic

Main Idea   Main Idea   Main Idea

Text Types—Structures with Graphic Organizers

23 *Answer*

Sequence

Text Types—Structures with Graphic Organizers

24 *Question*
Which text structure would use this graphic organizer?

Topic A   Topic B

Points   Differences   Similarities   Differences

Conclusion

Text Types—Structures with Graphic Organizers

24 *Answer*

Compare and Contrast

Text Types—Structures with Graphic Organizers

Text Types—Structures
with Graphic Organizers (continued)

Directions: Copy enough cards so each student receives a card. Cut out the cards on the dotted line. Fold cards on solid line and tape or glue the Question and Answer card back to back.

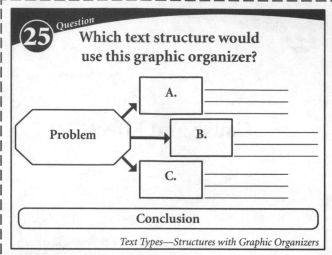

25 Question
Which text structure would use this graphic organizer?

Text Types—Structures with Graphic Organizers

25 Answer

Problem and Solution

Text Types—Structures with Graphic Organizers

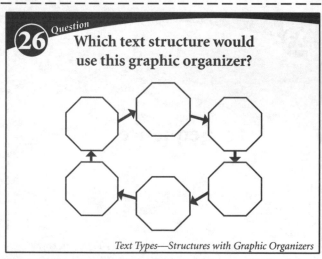

26 Question
Which text structure would use this graphic organizer?

Text Types—Structures with Graphic Organizers

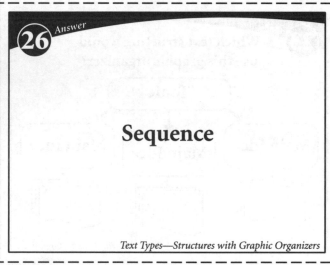

26 Answer

Sequence

Text Types—Structures with Graphic Organizers

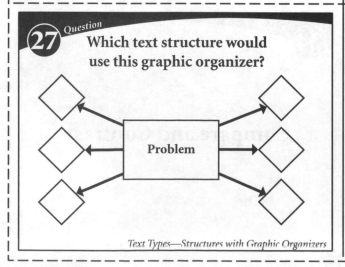

27 Question
Which text structure would use this graphic organizer?

Text Types—Structures with Graphic Organizers

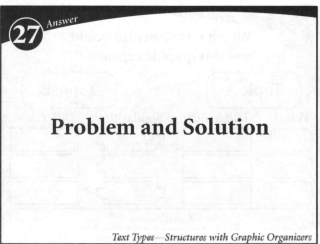

27 Answer

Problem and Solution

Text Types—Structures with Graphic Organizers

Text Types—Structures with Graphic Organizers (continued)

Directions: Copy enough cards so each student receives a card. Cut out the cards on the dotted line. Fold cards on solid line and tape or glue the Question and Answer card back to back.

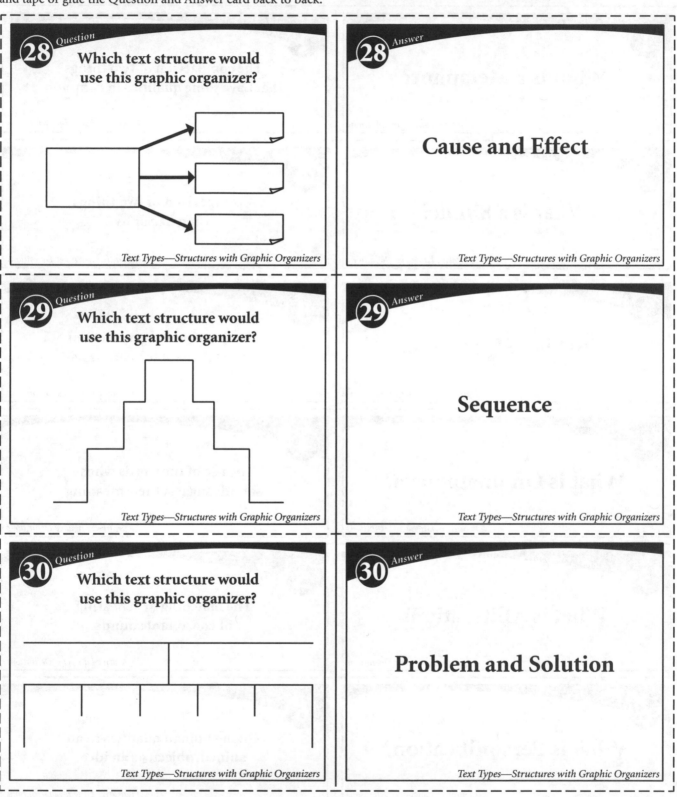

28 Question

Which text structure would use this graphic organizer?

Text Types—Structures with Graphic Organizers

28 Answer

Cause and Effect

Text Types—Structures with Graphic Organizers

29 Question

Which text structure would use this graphic organizer?

Text Types—Structures with Graphic Organizers

29 Answer

Sequence

Text Types—Structures with Graphic Organizers

30 Question

Which text structure would use this graphic organizer?

Text Types—Structures with Graphic Organizers

30 Answer

Problem and Solution

Text Types—Structures with Graphic Organizers

Figurative Language
Definitions

Directions: Copy enough cards so each student receives a card. Cut out the cards on the dotted line. Fold cards on solid line and tape or glue the Question and Answer card back to back.

1 Question

What is a Metaphor?

Figurative Language Definitions

1 Answer

The comparison of two things that have some qualities in common

Figurative Language Definitions

2 Question

What is a Simile?

Figurative Language Definitions

2 Answer

A comparison of two things using *like* or *as*

Figurative Language Definitions

3 Question

What is a Hyperbole?

Figurative Language Definitions

3 Answer

The use of an exaggeration or overstatement for emphasis

Figurative Language Definitions

4 Question

What is Onomatopoeia?

Figurative Language Definitions

4 Answer

The use of the words whose sounds suggest their meaning

Figurative Language Definitions

5 Question

What is Alliteration?

Figurative Language Definitions

5 Answer

The matching or repeating of consonant sounds

Figurative Language Definitions

6 Question

What is Personification?

Figurative Language Definitions

6 Answer

Giving human qualities to an animal, object, or an idea

Figurative Language Definitions

Figurative Language
Definitions *(continued)*

Directions: Copy enough cards so each student receives a card. Cut out the cards on the dotted line. Fold cards on solid line and tape or glue the Question and Answer card back to back.

7 Question **What is an Idiom?** *Figurative Language Definitions*	**7** Answer **A saying that has a special meaning that cannot be understood from the meaning of the individual words in the saying** *Figurative Language Definitions*
8 Question **What is Analogy?** *Figurative Language Definitions*	**8** Answer **A point-by-point comparison between two unlike things made to clarify one of the items** *Figurative Language Definitions*
9 Question **What is Imagery?** *Figurative Language Definitions*	**9** Answer **Mental images or a product of the imagination** *Figurative Language Definitions*
10 Question **What is Symbolism?** *Figurative Language Definitions*	**10** Answer **Objects used to represent other things or ideas** *Figurative Language Definitions*
11 Question **What is Assonance?** *Figurative Language Definitions*	**11** Answer **Repeated vowel sounds** *Figurative Language Definitions*
12 Question **What is a Cliché?** *Figurative Language Definitions*	**12** Answer **A word or phrase that has become overly familiar or commonplace** *Figurative Language Definitions*

Figurative Language
Definitions *(continued)*

Directions: Copy enough cards so each student receives a card. Cut out the cards on the dotted line. Fold cards on solid line and tape or glue the Question and Answer card back to back.

13 Question **What is Antithesis?** *Figurative Language Definitions*	**13** Answer **Saying the opposite of what you really mean to get an effect** *Figurative Language Definitions*
14 Question **What is an Oxymoron?** *Figurative Language Definitions*	**14** Answer **Successive words that seem to contradict each other** *Figurative Language Definitions*
15 Question **The use of objects to represent things or ideas in a literary work is an example of _____.** *Figurative Language Definitions*	**15** Answer **Symbolism** *Figurative Language Definitions*
16 Question **Giving human qualities to an animal, object, or an idea is an example of _____.** *Figurative Language Definitions*	**16** Answer **Personification** *Figurative Language Definitions*
17 Question **A saying that does not mean what it literally says is an example of _____.** *Figurative Language Definitions*	**17** Answer **Idiom** *Figurative Language Definitions*
18 Question **A point-by-point comparison between two unlike things, which helps to clarify one of the items, is an example of _____.** *Figurative Language Definitions*	**18** Answer **Analogy** *Figurative Language Definitions*

Figurative Language
Definitions (continued)

Directions: Copy enough cards so each student receives a card. Cut out the cards on the dotted line. Fold cards on solid line and tape or glue the Question and Answer card back to back.

19 Question
Mental images as a product of one's imagination are an example of _____.
Figurative Language Definitions

19 Answer
Imagery
Figurative Language Definitions

20 Question
Successive words that seem to contradict each other are called an _____.
Figurative Language Definitions

20 Answer
Oxymoron
Figurative Language Definitions

21 Question
The matching or repeating of consonant sounds is an example of _____.
Figurative Language Definitions

21 Answer
Alliteration
Figurative Language Definitions

22 Question
The repeating of vowel sounds is an example of _____.
Figurative Language Definitions

22 Answer
Assonance
Figurative Language Definitions

23 Question
Comparing two things that have some qualities in common is an example of _____.
Figurative Language Definitions

23 Answer
Metaphor
Figurative Language Definitions

24 Question
A comparison of two things using *like* or *as* is an example of _____.
Figurative Language Definitions

24 Answer
Simile
Figurative Language Definitions

Figurative Language
Definitions (continued)

Directions: Copy enough cards so each student receives a card. Cut out the cards on the dotted line. Fold cards on solid line and tape or glue the Question and Answer card back to back.

25 Question
Using a word or phrase that has become overly familiar or commonplace is called _____.

25 Answer
Cliché
Figurative Language Definitions

26 Question
Saying the opposite of what you really mean to get an effect is called _____.

26 Answer
Antithesis
Figurative Language Definitions

27 Question
The use of exaggeration or overstatement for emphasis is an example of _____.

27 Answer
Hyperbole
Figurative Language Definitions

28 Question
The use of words whose sounds suggest their meaning is an example of _____.

28 Answer
Onomatopoeia
Figurative Language Definitions

29 Question
_____ is a statement or opinion that seems contrary to a commonly accepted opinion.

29 Answer
Paradox
Figurative Language Definitions

30 Question

30 Answer
Figurative Language Definitions

Figurative Language
Examples

Directions: Copy enough cards so each student receives a card. Cut out the cards on the dotted line. Fold cards on solid line and tape or glue the Question and Answer card back to back.

1 *Question*

The clouds are marshmallow puffs in the sky.

This is an example of:
- **Idiom**
- **Onomatopoeia**
- **Metaphor**

Figurative Language Examples

---

1 *Answer*

Metaphor

Figurative Language Examples

---

2 *Question*

She sells seashells by the seashore.

This is an example of:
- **Personification**
- **Alliteration**
- **Simile**

Figurative Language Examples

---

2 *Answer*

Alliteration

Figurative Language Examples

---

3 *Question*

The water on the lake looked as smooth as glass.

This is an example of:
- **Simile**
- **Alliteration**
- **Imagery**

Figurative Language Examples

---

3 *Answer*

Simile

Figurative Language Examples

Figurative Language
Examples *(continued)*

Directions: Copy enough cards so each student receives a card. Cut out the cards on the dotted line. Fold cards on solid line and tape or glue the Question and Answer card back to back.

 Question

A green snake hissed as it slithered in the grass.

This is an example of:
- **Alliteration**
- **Onomatopoeia**
- **Metaphor**

Figurative Language Examples

 Answer

Onomatopoeia

Figurative Language Examples

 Question

I've told you a million times to clean your room.

This is an example of:
- **Hyperbole**
- **Alliteration**
- **Idiom**

Figurative Language Examples

5 **Answer**

Hyperbole

Figurative Language Examples

 Question

The dew was like a blanket of snow covering the land.

This is an example of:
- **Simile**
- **Metaphor**
- **Alliteration**

Figurative Language Examples

6 **Answer**

Simile

Figurative Language Examples

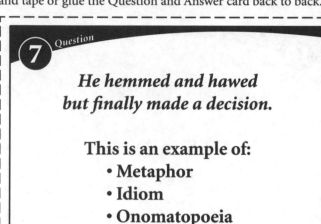

Figurative Language
Examples (continued)

Directions: Copy enough cards so each student receives a card. Cut out the cards on the dotted line. Fold cards on solid line and tape or glue the Question and Answer card back to back.

---

7 Question

He hemmed and hawed but finally made a decision.

This is an example of:
- **Metaphor**
- **Idiom**
- **Onomatopoeia**

Figurative Language Examples

---

7 Answer

Idiom

Figurative Language Examples

---

8 Question

Bobby Black buys bushels of blueberries.

This is an example of:
- **Personification**
- **Alliteration**
- **Metaphor**

Figurative Language Examples

---

8 Answer

Alliteration

Figurative Language Examples

---

9 Question

Fred Friday flipped five flat flapjacks.

This is an example of:
- **Simile**
- **Onomatopoeia**
- **Alliteration**

Figurative Language Examples

---

9 Answer

Alliteration

Figurative Language Examples

Figurative Language
Examples *(continued)*

Directions: Copy enough cards so each student receives a card. Cut out the cards on the dotted line. Fold cards on solid line and tape or glue the Question and Answer card back to back.

 Question

When the final buzzer rang, the overjoyed fans flooded the court like water from a wild faucet.

This is an example of:
- Alliteration
- Idiom
- Simile

Figurative Language Examples

 Answer

Simile

Figurative Language Examples

 Question

I'm so hungry I could eat a horse.

This is an example of:
- Metaphor
- Hyperbole
- Personification

Figurative Language Examples

 Answer

Hyperbole

Figurative Language Examples

 Question

The road was a ribbon of moon-light guiding us on our way home.

This is an example of:
- Imagery
- Metaphor
- Alliteration

Figurative Language Examples

 Answer

Metaphor

Figurative Language Examples

Figurative Language
Examples *(continued)*

Directions: Copy enough cards so each student receives a card. Cut out the cards on the dotted line. Fold cards on solid line and tape or glue the Question and Answer card back to back.

---

13 Question

Her eyes sparkled like the sunny sky as she received her award.

This is an example of:
- **Simile**
- **Hyperbole**
- **Onomatopoeia**

Figurative Language Examples

---

13 Answer

Simile

Figurative Language Examples

---

14 Question

The wild and wooly walrus wails and waddles while we wander wearily.

This is an example of:
- **Alliteration**
- **Imagery**
- **Metaphor**

Figurative Language Examples

---

14 Answer

Alliteration

Figurative Language Examples

---

15 Question

He was so surprised you could have knocked him over with a feather.

This is an example of:
- **Hyperbole**
- **Personification**
- **Imagery**

Figurative Language Examples

---

15 Answer

Hyperbole

Figurative Language Examples

Figurative Language
Examples *(continued)*

Directions: Copy enough cards so each student receives a card. Cut out the cards on the dotted line. Fold cards on solid line and tape or glue the Question and Answer card back to back.

16 Question

The poorest man is the richest, while the rich are poor.

This is an example of:
- **Metaphor**
- **Paradox**
- **Imagery**

Figurative Language Examples

16 Answer

Paradox

Figurative Language Examples

17 Question

Birds of a feather flock together.

This is an example of:
- **Idiom**
- **Hyperbole**
- **Metaphor**

Figurative Language Examples

17 Answer

Metaphor

Figurative Language Examples

18 Question

The rose wept.

This is an example of:
- **Metaphor**
- **Personification**
- **Imagery**

Figurative Language Examples

18 Answer

Personification

Figurative Language Examples

Figurative Language
Examples *(continued)*

Directions: Copy enough cards so each student receives a card. Cut out the cards on the dotted line. Fold cards on solid line and tape or glue the Question and Answer card back to back.

19 *Question*

Please hold your horses.

This is an example of:
- Imagery
- Idiom
- Onomatopoeia

Figurative Language Examples

19 *Answer*

Idiom

Figurative Language Examples

20 *Question*

The rain kissed her cheeks as it fell from the sky.

This is an example of:
- Personification
- Imagery
- Metaphor

Figurative Language Examples

20 *Answer*

Personification

Figurative Language Examples

21 *Question*

War is peace.

This is an example of:
- Alliteration
- Imagery
- Paradox

Figurative Language Examples

21 *Answer*

Paradox

Figurative Language Examples

Figurative Language
Examples *(continued)*

Directions: Copy enough cards so each student receives a card. Cut out the cards on the dotted line. Fold cards on solid line and tape or glue the Question and Answer card back to back.

---

22 *Question*

The slimy pumpkin seeds slid through my fingers.

This is an example of:
- **Personification**
- **Simile**
- **Imagery**

Figurative Language Examples

---

22 *Answer*

Imagery

Figurative Language Examples

---

23 *Question*

Her teeth are white pearls gleaming in the sunlight.

This is an example of:
- **Simile**
- **Metaphor**
- **Idiom**

Figurative Language Examples

---

23 *Answer*

Metaphor

Figurative Language Examples

---

24 *Question*

The bright rust and gold of the trees glimmered down the lane as we sped along on our bicycles.

This is an example of:
- **Imagery**
- **Metaphor**
- **Personification**

Figurative Language Examples

---

24 *Answer*

Imagery

Figurative Language Examples

Figurative Language
Examples *(continued)*

Directions: Copy enough cards so each student receives a card. Cut out the cards on the dotted line. Fold cards on solid line and tape or glue the Question and Answer card back to back.

25 *Question*

The fire crackled as we gazed into its bright light.

This is an example of:
- **Imagery**
- **Personification**
- **Onomatopoeia**

Figurative Language Examples

25 *Answer*

Onomatopoeia

Figurative Language Examples

26 *Question*

There are times when I think my computer hates me.

This is an example of:
- **Personification**
- **Metaphor**
- **Idiom**

Figurative Language Examples

26 *Answer*

Personification

Figurative Language Examples

27 *Question*

Sometimes things we read can be easily understood yet incomprehensible.

This is an example of:
- **Imagery**
- **Alliteration**
- **Paradox**

Figurative Language Examples

27 *Answer*

Paradox

Figurative Language Examples

Figurative Language
Examples *(continued)*

Directions: Copy enough cards so each student receives a card. Cut out the cards on the dotted line. Fold cards on solid line and tape or glue the Question and Answer card back to back.

(28) Question

The train was going clickity clack as it flashed across the old iron rail crossings.

This is an example of:
- Imagery
- Simile
- Onomatopoeia

Figurative Language Examples

(28) Answer

Onomatopoeia

Figurative Language Examples

(29) Question

I wouldn't believe everything he tells you; he's probably just pulling your leg.

This is an example of:
- Idiom
- Alliteration
- Hyperbole

Figurative Language Examples

(29) Answer

Idiom

Figurative Language Examples

(30) Question

Red and black jerseys crossed into the end zone to score the winning goal.

This is an example of:
- Imagery
- Metaphor
- Hyperbole

Figurative Language Examples

(30) Answer

Imagery

Figurative Language Examples

Homophones

Homophones *are words that are pronounced the same, but have different meanings.*

Directions: Copy enough cards so each student receives a card. Cut out the cards on the dotted line. Fold cards on solid line and tape or glue the Question and Answer card back to back.

---

1 Question
What is the difference between these homophones:
1. Flower
2. Flour
Homophones

1 Answer
*1. **Flower:** the blossom on a plant
2. **Flour:** a baking ingredient in pastry*
Homophones

---

2 Question
What is the difference between these homophones:
1. Meet
2. Meat
Homophones

2 Answer
*1. **Meet:** to gather at a determined location or time
2. **Meat:** the flesh of an animal*
Homophones

---

3 Question
What is the difference between these homophones:
1. Threw
2. Through
Homophones

3 Answer
*1. **Threw:** to toss with a ball
2. **Through:** to move to another place*
Homophones

---

4 Question
What is the difference between these homophones:
1. Ceiling
2. Sealing
Homophones

4 Answer
*1. **Ceiling:** the top part of a room
2. **Sealing:** to close something tightly*
Homophones

---

5 Question
What is the difference between these homophones:
1. Lesson
2. Lessen
Homophones

5 Answer
*1. **Lesson:** material studied and learned
2. **Lessen:** to diminish*
Homophones

---

6 Question
What is the difference between these homophones:
1. Whole
2. Hole
Homophones

6 Answer
*1. **Whole:** the entire piece
2. **Hole:** an opening in the ground*
Homophones

Homophones (continued)

Homophones *are words that are pronounced the same, but have different meanings.*

Directions: Copy enough cards so each student receives a card. Cut out the cards on the dotted line. Fold cards on solid line and tape or glue the Question and Answer card back to back.

7 Question
What is the difference between these homophones:
1. Side
2. Sighed
Homophones

7 Answer
1. Side: a position to the left or right of something
2. Sighed: an action word showing emotion
Homophones

8 Question
What is the difference between these homophones:
1. Blew
2. Blue
Homophones

8 Answer
1. Blew: an action word showing movement of air
2. Blue: a color
Homophones

9 Question
What is the difference between these homophones:
1. Herd
2. Heard
Homophones

9 Answer
1. Herd: a group of animals such as cows
2. Heard: a sound recognized by the ear
Homophones

10 Question
What is the difference between these homophones:
1. Minor
2. Miner
Homophones

10 Answer
1. Minor: a key in music
2. Miner: a worker in a mine
Homophones

11 Question
What is the difference between these homophones:
1. Dear
2. Deer
Homophones

11 Answer
1. Dear: an address used in writing a personal letter
2. Deer: a four-legged animal
Homophones

12 Question
What is the difference between these homophones:
1. Feet
2. Feat
Homophones

12 Answer
1. Feet: appendages at the end of one's legs
2. Feat: an achievement that requires great courage
Homophones

Homophones (continued)

Homophones *are words that are pronounced the same, but have different meanings.*

Directions: Copy enough cards so each student receives a card. Cut out the cards on the dotted line. Fold cards on solid line and tape or glue the Question and Answer card back to back.

13 *Question* **What is the difference between these homophones:**

1. Sees

2. Seas

Homophones

13 *Answer*

1. Sees: when one views images with the eyes
2. Seas: large bodies of water

Homophones

14 *Question* **What is the difference between these homophones:**

1. Steal

2. Steel

Homophones

14 *Answer*

1. Steal: to take something without permission that belongs to someone else
2. Steel: a heavy metal

Homophones

15 *Question* **What is the difference between these homophones:**

1. Some

2. Sum

Homophones

15 *Answer*

1. Some: referring to part of something
2. Sum: the answer to a math addition problem

Homophones

16 *Question* **What is the difference between these homophones:**

1. Pale

2. Pail

Homophones

16 *Answer*

1. Pale: the color of one's appearance when one feels ill
2. Pail: a container used to hold items

Homophones

17 *Question* **What is the difference between these homophones:**

1. Seen

2. Scene

Homophones

17 *Answer*

1. Seen: the past tense verb of seeing something
2. Scene: the place where an incident in real life or fiction occurs

Homophones

18 *Question* **What is the difference between these homophones:**

1. Waste

2. Waist

Homophones

18 *Answer*

1. Waste: material that is discarded
2. Waist: the area above the hips and below the diaphragm

Homophones

Homophones (continued)

Homophones *are words that are pronounced the same, but have different meanings.*
Directions: Copy enough cards so each student receives a card. Cut out the cards on the dotted line. Fold cards on solid line and tape or glue the Question and Answer card back to back.

19 Question
What is the difference between these homophones:
1. Road
2. Rode
Homophones

19 Answer
1. Road: a path to drive on
2. Rode: a past tense verb saying that you have traveled a distance
Homophones

20 Question
What is the difference between these homophones:
1. Flew
2. Flu
Homophones

20 Answer
1. Flew: to move through the air past tense, action verb to fly
2. Flu: an illness of an upset stomach
Homophones

21 Question
What is the difference between these homophones:
1. Made
2. Maid
Homophones

21 Answer
1. Made: to form something by putting parts together
2. Maid: someone hired to clean a house or building for someone else
Homophones

22 Question
What is the difference between these homophones:
1. Nose
2. Knows
Homophones

22 Answer
1. Nose: an extension on the face used for smelling
2. Knows: shows that one understands content
Homophones

23 Question
What is the difference between these homophones:
1. Hall
2. Haul
Homophones

23 Answer
1. Hall: a passageway between rooms
2. Haul: to carry something away
Homophones

24 Question
What is the difference between these homophones:
1. Break
2. Brake
Homophones

24 Answer
1. Break: to shatter into pieces
2. Brake: the stop pedal on a vehicle
Homophones

Homophones (continued)

Homophones *are words that are pronounced the same, but have different meanings.*

Directions: Copy enough cards so each student receives a card. Cut out the cards on the dotted line. Fold cards on solid line and tape or glue the Question and Answer card back to back.

25 Question
What is the difference between these homophones:
1. Hire
2. Higher
Homophones

25 Answer
1. Hire: to pay someone to work for you
2. Higher: a vertical distance
Homophones

26 Question
What is the difference between these homophones:
1. Weather
2. Whether
Homophones

26 Answer
1. Weather: the outdoor temperature
2. Whether: making a choice or decision
Homophones

27 Question
What is the difference between these homophones:
1. Pair
2. Pare
Homophones

27 Answer
1. Pair: two of anything
2. Pare: to peel such as an apple or pear
Homophones

28 Question
What is the difference between these homophones:
1. Bare
2. Bear
Homophones

28 Answer
1. Bare: empty such as a bare shelf
2. Bear: an animal that hibernates
Homophones

29 Question
What is the difference between these homophones:
1. Cent
2. Scent
Homophones

29 Answer
1. Cent: one penny
2. Scent: a distinctive smell
Homophones

30 Question
What is the difference between these homophones:
1. Die
2. Dye
Homophones

30 Answer
1. Die: to stop living
2. Dye: to change the color of something
Homophones

Homophones (continued)

Homophones *are words that are pronounced the same, but have different meanings.*

Directions: Copy enough cards so each student receives a card. Cut out the cards on the dotted line. Fold cards on solid line and tape or glue the Question and Answer card back to back.

31 Question
What is the difference between these homophones:
1. *Mail*
2. *Male*
Homophones

31 Answer
1. *Mail:* letters and packages delivered by the postal system to an address
2. *Male:* relates to characteristics of men
Homophones

32 Question
What is the difference between these homophones:
1. *Piece*
2. *Peace*
Homophones

32 Answer
1. *Piece:* part of something
2. *Peace:* a sense of tranquility
Homophones

33 Question
What is the difference between these homophones:
1. *Cereal*
2. *Serial*
Homophones

33 Answer
1. *Cereal:* a breakfast food
2. *Serial:* a number determining information
Homophones

34 Question
What is the difference between these homophones:
1. *Pause*
2. *Paws*
Homophones

34 Answer
1. *Pause:* to stop for a brief period of time
2. *Paws:* the padded feet of animals such as bears
Homophones

35 Question
What is the difference between these homophones:
1. *Wait*
2. *Weight*
Homophones

35 Answer
1. *Wait:* the time that passes before one gets something
2. *Weight:* the heaviness of an object
Homophones

36 Question
What is the difference between these homophones:
1. *Tale*
2. *Tail*
Homophones

36 Answer
1. *Tale:* a story that is not true but may sound true
2. *Tail:* the rear extension of an animal as on a dog
Homophones

Homophones *(continued)*

Homophones *are words that are pronounced the same, but have different meanings.*

Directions: Copy enough cards so each student receives a card. Cut out the cards on the dotted line. Fold cards on solid line and tape or glue the Question and Answer card back to back.

---

37 Question
What is the difference between these homophones:

1. Sale

2. Sail

Homophones

37 Answer

1. Sale: a reduction in price of an item
2. Sail: to ride in a boat on water

Homophones

---

38 Question

Homophones

38 Answer

Homophones

---

39 Question

Homophones

39 Answer

Homophones

---

40 Question

Homophones

40 Answer

Homophones

---

41 Question

Homophones

41 Answer

Homophones

---

42 Question

Homophones

42 Answer

Homophones

Blank Cards Template

Teacher Directions: Use this blank card template to make your own cards for Quiz-Quiz-Trade.

Question	Answer
Question	Answer
Question	Answer
Question	Answer
Question	Answer
Question	Answer

RallyCoach
Structure 4

Structure 4

RallyCoach

Partners take turns, one solving a problem while the other coaches.

Group Size
Pairs

Steps

Setup: Each pair needs one set of high-consensus problems and one pencil.

1 **Partner A Solves**
Partner A solves the first problem. When appropriate, Partner A expresses his or her thinking out loud so his or her partner can hear his or her ideas of thinking process.

2 **Partner B Coaches**
Partner B watches and listens, checks, coaches if necessary, and praises.

3 **Partner B Solves**
Partner B solves the next problem. When appropriate, Partner B expresses his or her thinking out loud so his or her partner can hear his or her ideas of thinking process.

4 **Partner A Coaches**
Partner A watches and listens, checks, coaches if necessary, and praises.

5 **Continue Solving**
Partners repeat taking turns solving successive problems.

Variation:
Pairs Check.
After solving two problems, pairs check their answers with the other pair in their team.

Tips
• Use a RallyCoach worksheet with problems labeled A and B.

Activities

Characterization Blank Worksheet Template...186

Vocabulary Words Blank Worksheet Template...191

Story Questions Blank Worksheet Template...192

RallyCoach Blank Worksheet Template...193

Idioms and Meanings

Directions: Copy a handout for each pair of students. Partners take turns defining the meaning of each idiom, orally explaining their thinking.

Partner (A)	Partner (B)
❶ Idiom *Just around the corner*	**❷ Idiom** *Keep at bay*
Meaning: _____	Meaning: _____
❸ Idiom *Keep it under your hat*	**❹ Idiom** *Keep mum*
Meaning: _____	Meaning: _____
❺ Idiom *Lay down the law*	**❻ Idiom** *Lame duck*
Meaning: _____	Meaning: _____

Idioms and Meanings *(continued)*

Directions: Copy a handout for each pair of students. Partners take turns defining the meaning of each idiom, orally explaining their thinking.

Partner Ⓐ	Partner Ⓑ

❼ **Idiom**
Made in the shade

Meaning: _____

_____

_____

_____

_____

❽ **Idiom**
Make my day

Meaning: _____

_____

_____

_____

_____

❾ **Idiom**
Have a nest egg

Meaning: _____

_____

_____

_____

_____

❿ **Idiom**
The nitty gritty

Meaning: _____

_____

_____

_____

_____

⓫ **Idiom**
Off the cuff

Meaning: _____

_____

_____

_____

⓬ **Idiom**
On the lam

Meaning: _____

_____

_____

_____

Idioms and Meanings *(continued)*

Directions: Copy a handout for each pair of students. Partners take turns defining the meaning of each idiom, orally explaining their thinking.

Partner Ⓐ	Partner Ⓑ

⑬
Idiom
The up and up

Meaning: _____

_____

_____

_____

_____

⑭
Idiom
On your soapbox

Meaning: _____

_____

_____

_____

_____

⑮
Idiom
Packed in like sardines

Meaning: _____

_____

_____

_____

_____

⑯
Idiom
Pay through the nose

Meaning: _____

_____

_____

_____

_____

⑰
Idiom
Pick up the tab

Meaning: _____

_____

_____

_____

⑱
Idiom
Quick as a flash

Meaning: _____

_____

_____

_____

Idioms and Meanings *(continued)*

Directions: Copy a handout for each pair of students. Partners take turns defining the meaning of each idiom, orally explaining their thinking.

Partner (A)	Partner (B)

19 **Idiom**
Quick on the trigger

Meaning: _____
_____
_____
_____
_____

20 **Idiom**
Rake someone over the coals

Meaning: _____
_____
_____
_____
_____

21 **Idiom**
Recharge your batteries

Meaning: _____
_____
_____
_____
_____

22 **Idiom**
Save your skin

Meaning: _____
_____
_____
_____
_____

23 **Idiom**
Seeing eye to eye

Meaning: _____
_____
_____
_____

24 **Idiom**
Taking it on the chin

Meaning: _____
_____
_____
_____

Idioms and Meanings (continued)

Directions: Copy a handout for each pair of students. Partners take turns defining the meaning of each idiom, orally explaining their thinking.

Partner Ⓐ	Partner Ⓑ

25 Idiom
To a T

Meaning: _____

_____

_____

_____

26 Idiom
Drop me a line

Meaning: _____

_____

_____

_____

27 Idiom
Let's call it a day

Meaning: _____

_____

_____

_____

28 Idiom
Hold your horses

Meaning: _____

_____

_____

_____

29 Idiom
Sounds like a plan

Meaning: _____

_____

_____

_____

30 Idiom
I'm pumped

Meaning: _____

_____

_____

_____

Idioms and Meanings (continued)

Directions: Copy a handout for each pair of students. Partners take turns defining the meaning of each idiom, orally explaining their thinking.

Partner Ⓐ	Partner Ⓑ
㉛ **Idiom** *Get the show on the road*	**㉜** **Idiom** *Get the short end of the stick*
Meaning: _____	Meaning: _____
_____	_____
_____	_____
_____	_____
㉝ **Idiom** *A dime a dozen*	**㉞** **Idiom** *A blessing in disguise*
Meaning: _____	Meaning: _____
_____	_____
_____	_____
_____	_____
㉟ **Idiom** *A fool and his money are soon parted*	**㊱** **Idiom** *A fair-weather friend*
Meaning: _____	Meaning: _____
_____	_____
_____	_____
_____	_____

Idioms and Meanings
Answer Key

Idioms & Meanings

1 **Idiom:** *Just around the corner*
Meaning: Something that is expected to happen soon

2 **Idiom:** *Keep at bay*
Meaning: Maintaining a safe distance from someone

3 **Idiom:** *Keep it under your hat*
Meaning: Keeping a secret

4 **Idiom:** *Keep mum*
Meaning: Keeping quiet and not passing on information

5 **Idiom:** *Lay down the law*
Meaning: Telling people what to do or acting as an authoritarian

6 **Idiom:** *Lame duck*
Meaning: Something or someone that is weak or lacks power

7 **Idiom:** *Made in the shade*
Meaning: The easy life

8 **Idiom:** *Make my day*
Meaning: Something making you happy

9 **Idiom:** *Have a nest egg*
Meaning: Saving money for the future

10 **Idiom:** *The nitty gritty*
Meaning: Focusing on the important issues

11 **Idiom:** *Off the cuff*
Meaning: Doing something without any preparation

12 **Idiom:** *On the lam*
Meaning: Hiding out from the authorities to avoid arrest or prison

13 **Idiom:** *The up and up*
Meaning: Someone being truthful about what they say and do

14 **Idiom:** *On your soapbox*
Meaning: Expresses someone's passion for a topic or issue

15 **Idiom:** *Packed in like sardines*
Meaning: Talking about being in a place that is extremely crowded

16 **Idiom:** *Pay through the nose*
Meaning: Paying a high price for something

17 **Idiom:** *Pick up the tab*
Meaning: Paying for everyone's meal at dinner or some other event

18 **Idiom:** *Quick as a flash*
Meaning: Saying that something happens very quickly

19 **Idiom:** *Quick on the trigger*
Meaning: Someone is quick to react

20 **Idiom:** *Rake someone over the coals*
Meaning: Scolding or criticizing someone severely

21 **Idiom:** *Recharge your batteries*
Meaning: Regaining your energy after working hard at something

Idioms and Meanings
Answer Key *(continued)*

Idioms & Meanings

22 **Idiom:** *Save your skin*
Meaning: Someone who manages to avoid getting into serious trouble

23 **Idiom:** *Seeing eye to eye*
Meaning: Agreeing on things or a situation

24 **Idiom:** *Taking it on the chin*
Meaning: Something bad happening to you that you deal with without the fuss

25 **Idiom:** *To a T*
Meaning: Something being done perfectly

26 **Idiom:** *Drop me a line*
Meaning: Writing a letter to someone

27 **Idiom:** *Let's call it a day*
Meaning: Saying we are finished with our work for today

28 **Idiom:** *Hold your horses*
Meaning: Not getting upset

29 **Idiom:** *Sounds like a plan*
Meaning: Something being a good idea

30 **Idiom:** *I'm pumped*
Meaning: Being excited about something

31 **Idiom:** *Get the show on the road*
Meaning: To get something started

32 **Idiom:** *Get the short end of the stick*
Meaning: To suffer the bad effects of a situation

33 **Idiom:** *A dime a dozen*
Meaning: Reducing the perceived value of something

34 **Idiom:** *A blessing in disguise*
Meaning: Something that seems like a problem but has an unexpected beneficial effect

35 **Idiom:** *A fool and his money are soon parted*
Meaning: A truism: stupidity costs money

36 **Idiom:** *A fair-weather friend*
Meaning: A person who is a friend during the good times but not the bad times

Suffixes

Directions: Copy the handout for each pair of students. Using RallyCoach, partners take turns writing appropriate words in the columns, and recording the word's meaning.

Words	Meanings
–ment **A** _____ **B** _____	**A** _____ _____ **B** _____ _____
–ation **A** _____ **B** _____	**A** _____ _____ **B** _____ _____
–ous **A** _____ **B** _____	**A** _____ _____ **B** _____ _____
–ible **A** _____ **B** _____	**A** _____ _____ **B** _____ _____
–ify **A** _____ **B** _____	**A** _____ _____ **B** _____ _____

Romeo and Juliet *Blackline*
Themes

Directions: : Copy a handout for each pair of students. Pairs find evidence in the play to support the theme ideas listed below. Students must list the evidence passage and page number from the text and explain why they selected the passage as evidence.

Theme Ideas		
Power of Love	**Love Causing Violence**	**Inevitability of Fate**
Ⓐ Evidence (page no.)	**Ⓐ Evidence (page no.)**	**Ⓐ Evidence (page no.)**
_____	_____	_____
_____	_____	_____
_____	_____	_____
Reason for Selection	**Reason for Selection**	**Reason for Selection**
_____	_____	_____
_____	_____	_____
_____	_____	_____
_____	_____	_____
_____	_____	_____
_____	_____	_____
_____	_____	_____
Ⓑ Evidence (page no.)	**Ⓑ Evidence (page no.)**	**Ⓑ Evidence (page no.)**
_____	_____	_____
_____	_____	_____
_____	_____	_____
Reason for Selection	**Reason for Selection**	**Reason for Selection**
_____	_____	_____
_____	_____	_____
_____	_____	_____
_____	_____	_____
_____	_____	_____
_____	_____	_____

The Pearl
Symbolism

Directions: Copy the handout for each pair of students. For each of the characters or items listed below, pairs determine the symbolism and in turn cite one piece of evidence and the page number from the novel that indicates whether the person or object is good or bad.

Symbolism

In the introduction to *The Pearl*, the reader is told the story contains "only good and bad things and black and white things and good and evil things and no in-between things."

A symbol is an object, action, or person used to represent itself as well as something else. For example, eagles are a type of bird, that also can stand for freedom. The meaning of symbols can change when a different character's viewpoint is considered, or as the story progresses.

The doctor symbolizes _____

A Evidence (page no.) _____

_____

_____

_____

B Evidence (page no.) _____

_____

_____

_____

The sea symbolizes _____

A Evidence (page no.) _____

_____

_____

_____

B Evidence (page no.) _____

_____

_____

_____

The Pearl
Symbolism *(continued)*

Directions: Copy the handout for each pair of students. For each of the characters or items listed below, pairs determine the symbolism and in turn cite one piece of evidence and the page number from the novel that indicates whether the person or object is good or bad.

Symbolism

The pearl buyers symbolize _____

A Evidence (page no.) _____

_____

_____

B Evidence (page no.) _____

_____

_____

The priest symbolizes _____

A Evidence (page no.) _____

_____

_____

B Evidence (page no.) _____

_____

_____

The rifle symbolizes _____

A Evidence (page no.) _____

_____

_____

B Evidence (page no.) _____

_____

_____

The Pearl
Characterization

Directions: Copy the handout for each pair of students. Using RallyCoach, pairs respond to the questions about *The Pearl*.

Characterization

Characterization is what a writer does to reveal the character for the reader. The writer accomplishes this through a description of the character's appearance, his or her inner thoughts and feelings, words or actions the character uses to convey thoughts and emotions, and the effect one character has on the other characters.

John Steinbeck's *The Pearl* provides examples of these techniques of characterization.

Partner A **1** Explain three specific things Kino does to show his character.	
Partner B **2** Identify two examples of Juana demonstrating she is a caring wife and mother.	
Partner A **3** The doctor reveals his character in two specific ways. Identify them.	

The Pearl
Characterization *(continued)*

Directions: Copy the handout for each pair of students. Using RallyCoach, pairs respond to the questions about *The Pearl*.

Characterization

Partner B

4

What do the "songs" Kino hears explain about him as a person?

Partner A

5

Record two specific reactions of other characters to the doctor.

Partner B

6

What major lessons can be learned from reading *The Pearl*?

Characterization
Blank Worksheet Template

Teacher Directions: Fill in the name of the novel or short story. Write questions about characterization. Copy the handout for eacher pair of students.

Characterization

Partner A **Question:**	**Answer:**
Partner B **Question:**	**Answer:**
Partner A **Question:**	**Answer:**
Partner B **Question:**	**Answer:**

Parts of Speech
Worksheet #1

Directions: Copy a handout for each pair of students. Using the word list, pairs take turns recording if the word is a noun, verb, adjective, or adverb by marking the correct column. Explain your answer.

Words to Sort	Noun	Verb	Adjective	Adverb	Reason
A Instill					
B Discern					
A Creed					
B Irate					
A Perpetual					
B Contend					
A Presume					
B Rote					
A Banish					
B Futile					
A Cynical					
B Extent					
A Divertingly					
B Gauge					
A Interval					
B Lenient					
A Fraternally					
B Hobble					

Parts of Speech
Worksheet #2

Directions: Copy a handout for each pair of students. Using the word list, pairs take turns recording if the word is a noun, verb, adjective, or adverb by marking the correct column. Explain your answer.

Words to Sort	Noun	Verb	Adjective	Adverb	Reason
A Momentum					
B Lament					
A Reproach					
B Resonate					
A Promenade					
B Intercession					
A Placate					
B Restitution					
A Protocol					
B Felicitous					
A Compelling					
B Blare					
A Flamboyant					
B Sinister					
A Transcend					
B Tread					
A Terse					
B Chronic					

Parts of Speech
Answer Key

Directions: Copy a handout for each pair. Pairs review the parts of speech and word list. Using the word list, pairs RallyCoach as they record the words as a noun, verb, adjective, or adverb in the correct column. Explain your answer.

Worksheet #1	Worksheet #2
Instill ....Verb	Momentum .... Noun
Discern ....Verb	Lament ....Verb
Creed .... Noun	Reproach .... Noun
Irate ....Adjective	Resonate...........................Verb
Perpetual..................Adjective	Promenade.................... Noun
Contend............................Verb	Intercession .... Noun
Presume ....Verb	Placate ....Verb
Rote................................. Noun	Restitution .... Noun
Banish ....Verb	Protocol.......................... Noun
Futile .... Adjective	Felicitous..................Adjective
Cynical......................Adjective	Compelling ....Adjective
Extent .... Noun	Blare .... Noun
Divertingly.................. Adverb	Flamboyant..............Adjective
Gauge.................................Verb	Sinister ....Adjective
Interval........................... Noun	Transcend.........................Verb
Lenient ....Adjective	Tread.................................Verb
Fraternally .... Adverb	Terse ....Adjective
Hobble ....Verb	Chronic ....Adjective

Vocabulary Words

Directions: Copy a handout for each pair of students. Partners RallyCoach to define the vocabulary word and create a sentence with its meaning.

Word	Definition	Sample Sentence
A Sedentary		
B Jettison		
A Extradite		
B Culminate		
A Flack		
B Voracious		
A Meticulous		
B Propensity		

Vocabulary Words
Blank Worksheet Template

Teacher Directions: Fill in vocabulary words from a novel or vocabulary list. Copy one worksheet per pair of students to define each word and provide a sample sentence using RallyCoach.

Word	Definition	Sample Sentence
A		
B		
A		
B		
A		
B		
A		
B		

Story Questions
Blank Worksheet Template

Teacher Directions: Fill in the name of the story. Write questions for partners to answer using RallyCoach. Copy one worksheet per pair.

Story _____

Partner A Question:	Answer:
Partner B Question:	Answer:
Partner A Question:	Answer:
Partner B Question:	Answer:
Partner A Question:	Answer:
Partner B Question:	Answer:

RallyCoach
Blank Worksheet Template

Teacher Directions: Use this blank worksheet to create your own worksheet to answer questions using RallyCoach. Copy one worksheet per pair.

Partner A	Partner B

Blank Worksheet Template

Directions: Copy enough cards for each student. Cut the cards, fold and glue the Question and Answer card back to back. Cards may be laminated for future uses.

Partner Ⓐ	Partner Ⓑ

RoundRobin
Structure 5

Structure 5

RoundRobin

In teams, students take turns responding orally.

Group Size
Teams of Four

Steps

1 **Teacher Assigns Task**
Teacher poses a problem to which there are multiple possible responses or solutions, and provides think time.

2 **Teammates Take Turns Responding**
Students take turns stating responses or solutions.

Tips

• When using RoundRobin with a cube, one student rolls the cube and answers the question. He or she passes the cube clockwise and the next student rolls the cube and answers.

• If the cube selects the same prompt for a different student, he or she must answer. If the cube selects the same prompt for the same student, he or she rolls again until he or she receives a new question or prompt.

Activities

Cubes: *Teacher gives each team a cube with questions for teams to use as discussion for any of the following:*

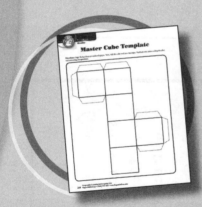

RoundRobin
Master Cube Template...205

Cause and Effect Cube

Directions: Copy the handout on cardstock paper. Cut out the cube along the outer line. Fold it into a cube and tape the edges. Teammates take turns rolling the cube and answering the questions.

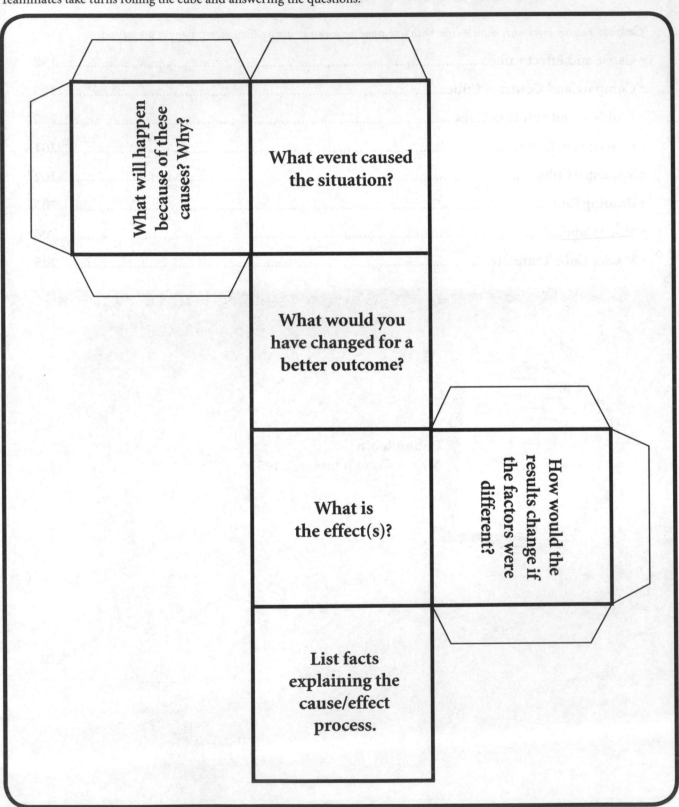

What will happen because of these causes? Why?

What event caused the situation?

What would you have changed for a better outcome?

What is the effect(s)?

How would the results change if the factors were different?

List facts explaining the cause/effect process.

Compare and Contrast Cube

Directions: Copy the handout on cardstock paper. Cut out the cube along the outer line. Fold it into a cube and tape the edges. Teammates take turns rolling the cube and answering the questions.

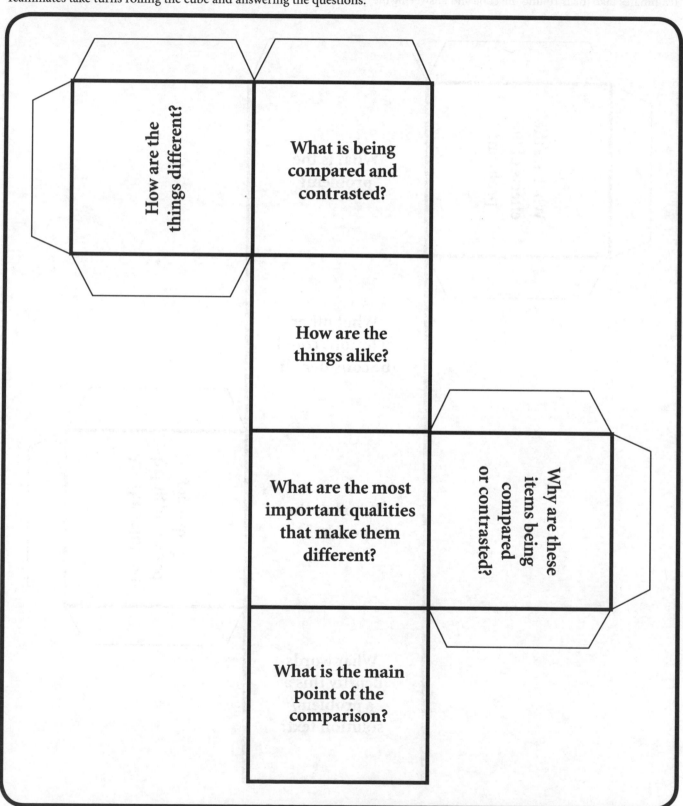

How are the things different?

What is being compared and contrasted?

How are the things alike?

What are the most important qualities that make them different?

Why are these items being compared or contrasted?

What is the main point of the comparison?

Problem and Solution Cube

Directions: Copy the handout on cardstock paper. Cut out the cube along the outer line. Fold it into a cube and tape the edges. Teammates take turns rolling the cube and answering the questions.

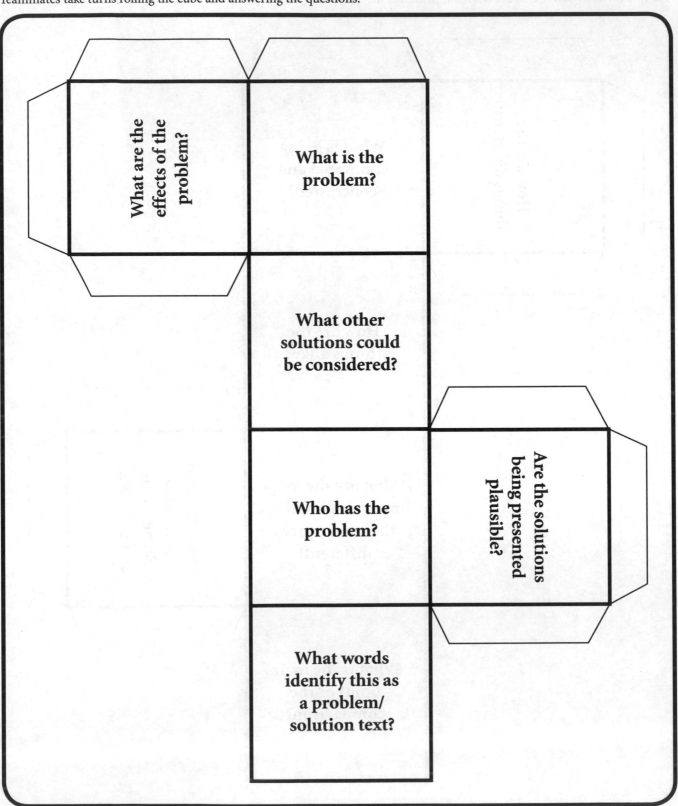

What are the effects of the problem?

What is the problem?

What other solutions could be considered?

Are the solutions being presented plausible?

Who has the problem?

What words identify this as a problem/ solution text?

Description Cube

Directions: Copy the handout on cardstock paper. Cut out the cube along the outer line. Fold it into a cube and tape the edges. Teammates take turns rolling the cube and answering the questions.

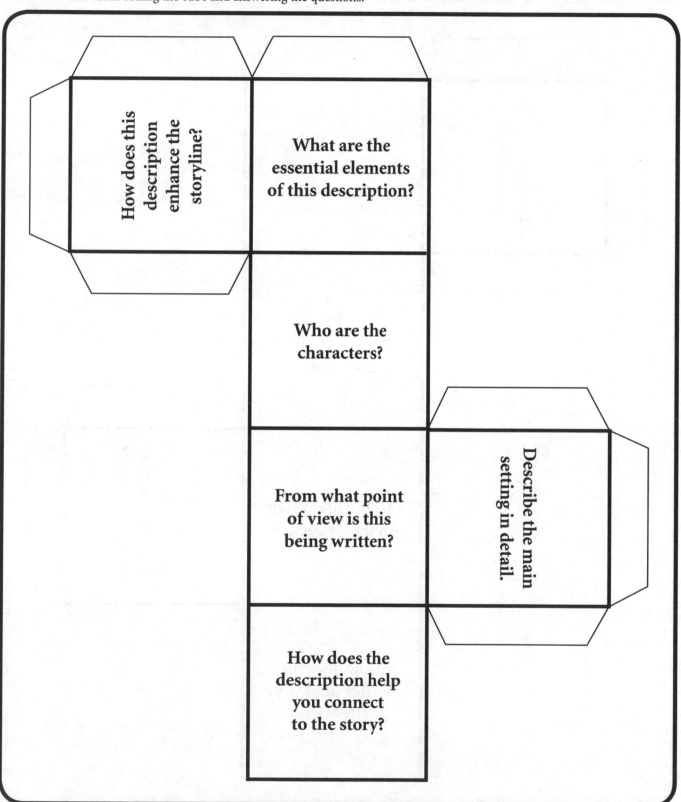

How does this description enhance the storyline?

What are the essential elements of this description?

Who are the characters?

From what point of view is this being written?

Describe the main setting in detail.

How does the description help you connect to the story?

Sequence Cube

Directions: Copy the handout on cardstock paper. Cut out the cube along the outer line. Fold it into a cube and tape the edges. Teammates take turns rolling the cube and answering the questions.

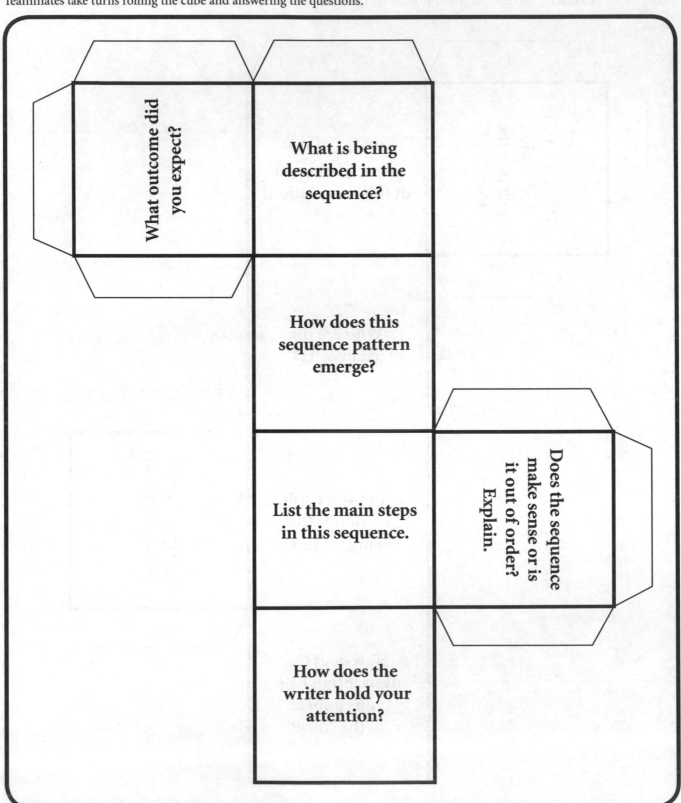

What outcome did you expect?

What is being described in the sequence?

How does this sequence pattern emerge?

List the main steps in this sequence.

Does the sequence make sense or is it out of order? Explain.

How does the writer hold your attention?

Reading Cube

Directions: Copy the handout on cardstock paper. Cut out the cube along the outer line. Fold it into a cube and tape the edges. Teammates take turns rolling the cube and answering the questions.

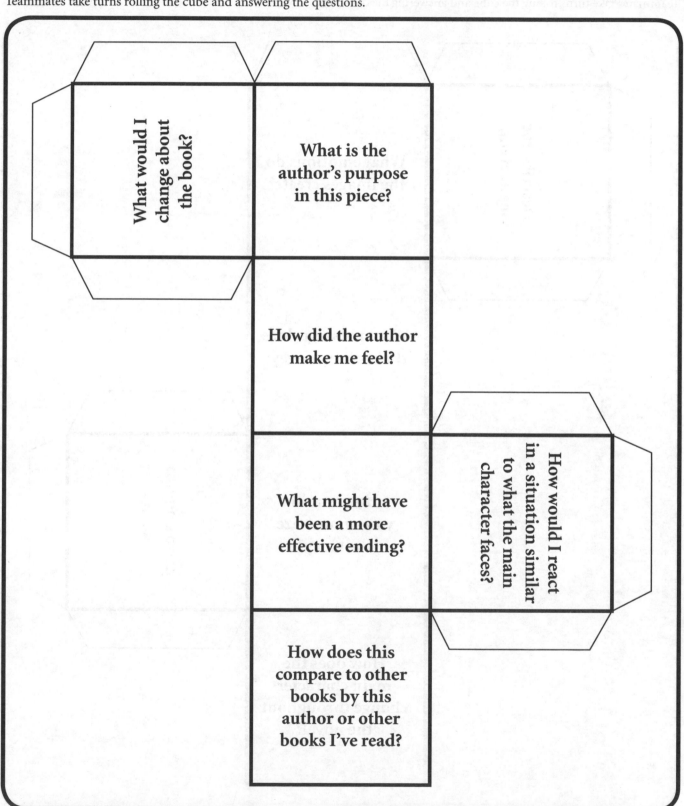

What would I change about the book?

What is the author's purpose in this piece?

How did the author make me feel?

What might have been a more effective ending?

How would I react in a situation similar to what the main character faces?

How does this compare to other books by this author or other books I've read?

Story Cube

Directions: Copy the handout on cardstock paper. Cut out the cube along the outer line. Fold it into a cube and tape the edges. Teammates take turns rolling the cube and answering the questions.

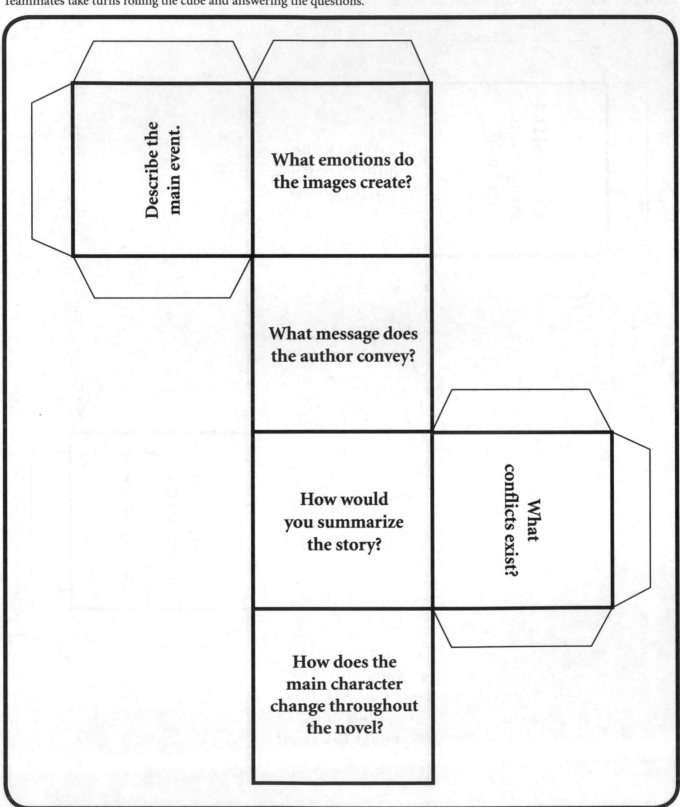

Describe the main event.

What emotions do the images create?

What message does the author convey?

How would you summarize the story?

What conflicts exist?

How does the main character change throughout the novel?

Master Cube Template

Teacher Directions: Fill in the six faces of the cube with a question or prompt on each face. Copy the handout on cardstock paper. Cut out the cube along the outer line. Fold it into a cube and tape the edges. Teammates take turns rolling the cube and answering the questions.

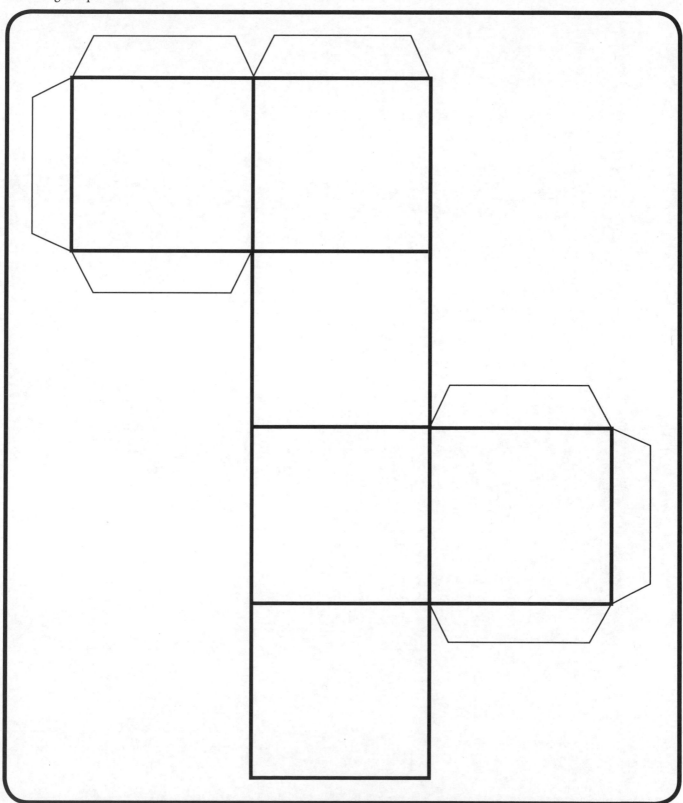

Teammates Consult
Structure 6

Structure 6

Teammates Consult

Students consult teammates to collect ideas and information on the topic, then record their own ideas.

Group Size
Teams of Four

Steps

Setup: Question cards may be used.

1 Students Number Off
Students number off from 1–4 and place their pens down in the center of the team area, or in a pencil cup.

2 Discussion Leader Reads First Question
Student #1, the Discussion Leader, reads the first question (or the question may be asked by the teacher).

3 Teammates Consult
Teammates discuss answers or ideas. To ensure everyone is participating, a rule can be established that the student to the right of the Discussion Leader must start the discussion.

4 Discussion Leader Checks for Understanding
The Discussion Leader checks to make sure all ideas are out and heard and students are ready to write their answers.

5 Students Write
The Discussion Leader calls, "Let's write." Students write their answers in their own words with no discussion.

6 Continue Consulting
When finished writing, teammates place pens in the center or pencil cup. The person on the left of the Discussion Leader becomes the next Discussion Leader for a new round.

Tips
• Teammates Consult does not work with one-word answers such as true or false or short answers. Teammates Consult works best with questions that require elaborate responses or else students will just give the answer rather than engage in a meaningful sharing of ideas.
• Place a cup, tub, or mug in the center of each team's table. Students place their pens or pencils in the cup during the consultation period so no one can work on the problem or write their response while consultation is in progress. No talking when the cup is empty!

Activities

**Any Novel—
Character Sketch...211**

Of Mice and Men
Character Sketch

Directions: In the character traits box, list Lennie's character traits. Teammates Consult: Share your list and pick one trait to describe in detail. Record any new traits you hear from teammates. When done, use your list to write your own character sketch of Lennie in the character sketch box. Take turns reading your character sketches to teammates.

Character Traits
Lennie

Character Sketch
Lennie

Any Novel
Character Sketch

Directions: In the character traits box, list the character's traits. Teammates Consult: Share your list and pick one trait to describe in detail. Record any new traits you hear from teammates. When done, use your list to write your own character sketch in the character sketch box. Take turns reading your character sketches to teammates.

Character _____

Character Traits

_____

_____

_____

_____

_____

_____

_____

Character Sketch

_____

_____

_____

_____

_____

_____

_____

_____

_____

A Tale of Two Cities
Discussion Prompts

Directions: In teams, discuss each prompt below without writing. When done discussing each question, write your own answer to the question.

1. What major themes appear in the novel? _____
   _____
   _____
   _____

2. What do we learn about the time period since the story takes place in two cities?_____
   _____
   _____
   _____
   _____

3. List the traits of Carton and Darnay. Place an asterisk beside any traits they have in common. _____
   _____
   _____
   _____

4. Carton repeats the biblical passage, "I am the resurrection and the life," as he walks through the city streets. What significance does this verse have on the decision he makes later to save Darnay? _____
   _____
   _____
   _____

5. List examples of foreshadowing. As a team, reach a consensus for three major examples of foreshadowing._____
   _____
   _____
   _____

6. What is the overall message Dickens is suggesting? What does he say about human behavior? _____
   _____
   _____
   _____

A Tale of Two Cities Discussion Prompts

Night
Timeline of Important Events

Directions: In teams, discuss the important events you can recall or locate for each time period. When done discussing each time period, record the events you can recall in your own words.

1930–1934

In early January 1930, eight Berlin Jews are murdered by storm troopers. Nazis hold 107 seats in Germany's parliament. Hitler rises to power. Nazis are declared a political party.

_____

_____

_____

_____

_____

_____

_____

_____

1935–1939

Jewish citizenship revoked. Germany allies with Italy and Japan. Jews forced into ghettos and many sent to concentration camps. Germany invades Poland.

_____

_____

_____

_____

_____

_____

_____

_____

1940–1943

Jews confined to ghettos. Japan bombs Pearl Harbor. United States enters war. Crematories open in Auschwitz. Allies pursue Nazis into Italy.

_____

_____

_____

_____

_____

_____

_____

_____

1944–1945

Jewish deportation continues. Jews must wear Star of David. Allies liberate Paris. Red Army liberates Auschwitz. Hitler commits suicide. Germany surrenders. World War II ends.

_____

_____

_____

_____

_____

_____

_____

_____

Idioms

Directions: Cut out the cards on the dotted line and fold cards on solid line. Place them in a pile with the questions facing up. Discuss the meaning of the Idiom as a team, then independently record your explanation on the recording sheet.

1 Question	**1 Answer**
Explain the meaning of the idiom: **seeing eye to eye.**	*Seeing eye to eye* means we are able to agree on an issue.
2 Question	**2 Answer**
Explain the meaning of the idiom: **off the record.**	If something is *off the record*, it is not to be recorded.
3 Question	**3 Answer**
Explain the meaning of the idiom: **take heart.**	To *take heart* means to be encouraged about whatever is happening or one is experiencing.
4 Question	**4 Answer**
Explain the meaning of the idiom: **bury the hatchet.**	To *bury the hatchet* means to make peace with someone or decide to forget about some concern.
5 Question	**5 Answer**
Explain the meaning of the idiom: **curiosity killed the cat.**	*Curiosity killed the cat* means being inquisitive may lead one into a dangerous situation.
6 Question	**6 Answer**
Explain the meaning of the idiom: **a far cry.**	*A far cry* means a long way or something of a great difference.

Idioms *(continued)*

Directions: Cut out the cards on the dotted line and fold cards on solid line. Place them in a pile with the questions facing up. Discuss the meaning of the Idiom as a team, then independently record your explanation on the recording sheet.

7 Question

Explain the meaning of the idiom:

that's that.

7 Answer

That's that means a matter is settled or has been decided.

8 Question

Explain the meaning of the idiom:

hit it off.

8 Answer

If you *hit it off*, you get along well together or tend to agree on most issues.

9 Question

Explain the meaning of the idiom:

bring home the bacon.

9 Answer

To *bring home the bacon* means to be successful or to win a prize.

10 Question

Explain the meaning of the idiom:

in full blast.

10 Answer

In full blast means to be in full operation as in a project.

11 Question

Explain the meaning of the idiom:

break a leg.

11 Answer

To *break a leg* is a superstitious way to say "good luck".

12 Question

Explain the meaning of the idiom:

let the cat out of the bag.

12 Answer

If you *let the cat out of the bag,* you are someone who has shared a secret that wasn't supposed to be shared.

Idioms (continued)

Directions: Cut out the cards on the dotted line and fold cards on solid line. Place them in a pile with the questions facing up. Discuss the meaning of the Idiom as a team, then independently record your explanation on the recording sheet.

13 Question

Explain the meaning of the idiom:
all in the same boat.

13 Answer

If you are *all in the same boat*, you are all facing the same challenges.

14 Question

Explain the meaning of the idiom:
water under the bridge.

14 Answer

Water under the bridge means anything from the past that has been a problem is no longer important.

15 Question

Explain the meaning of the idiom:
new kid on the block.

15 Answer

If you are the *new kid on the block*, you are new to the group or the area.

16 Question

Explain the meaning of the idiom:
the ball is in your court.

16 Answer

If *the ball is in your court*, it means that this time it is your decision.

17 Question

Explain the meaning of the idiom:
smell something fishy.

17 Answer

If you *smell something fishy*, you are detecting that something is not right.

18 Question

Explain the meaning of the idiom:
up a blind alley.

18 Answer

Up a blind alley means you may be going down a certain path that could lead to a bad outcome.

Idioms (continued)

Directions: Cut out the cards on the dotted line and fold cards on solid line. Place them in a pile with the questions facing up. Discuss the meaning of the Idiom as a team, then independently record your explanation on the recording sheet.

19 Question

Explain the meaning of the idiom:

you can't judge a book by its cover.

19 Answer

You can't judge a book by its cover means you should not make a decision based primarily on appearances.

20 Question

Explain the meaning of the idiom:

down to the wire.

20 Answer

Down to the wire means something that ends at the very last minute or the last few seconds.

21 Question

Explain the meaning of the idiom:

going the extra mile.

21 Answer

Going the extra mile means going above and beyond whatever is required for the task at hand.

22 Question

Explain the meaning of the idiom:

a piece of cake.

22 Answer

A piece of cake means that a task you are facing can easily be accomplished.

23 Question

Explain the meaning of the idiom:

jump through hoops.

23 Answer

To *jump through hoops* means to be willing to go to great lengths to do something well.

24 Question

Explain the meaning of the idiom:

go out on a limb.

24 Answer

To *go out on a limb* means someone may be heading into a risky situation.

Idioms Recording Sheet

Directions: Record your own explanation of each idiom below. After each idiom, compare your explanation with the explanation on the back of the card.

Teammates Consult Idioms Recording Worksheet

1. *Seeing eye to eye* _____
_____
_____
_____
_____

2. *Off the record* _____
_____
_____
_____
_____

3. *Take heart* _____
_____
_____
_____
_____

4. *Bury the hatchet* _____
_____
_____
_____
_____

5. *Curiosity killed the cat* _____
_____
_____
_____
_____

6. *A far cry* _____
_____
_____
_____
_____

7. *That's that* _____
_____
_____
_____
_____

8. *Hit it off* _____
_____
_____
_____
_____

9. *Bring home the bacon* _____
_____
_____
_____
_____

10. *In full blast* _____
_____
_____
_____
_____

11. *Break a leg* _____
_____
_____
_____
_____

12. *Let the cat out of the bag* _____
_____
_____
_____
_____

Idioms Recording Sheet *(continued)*

Directions: Record your own explanation of each idiom below. After each idiom, compare your explanation with the explanation on the back of the card.

Teammates Consult Idioms Recording Worksheet

13. *All in the same boat* _____

_____

_____

_____

_____

14. *Water under the bridge* _____

_____

_____

_____

_____

15. *New kid on the block* _____

_____

_____

_____

_____

16. *The ball is in your court* _____

_____

_____

_____

_____

17. *Smell something fishy* _____

_____

_____

_____

_____

18. *Up a blind alley* _____

_____

_____

_____

19. *You can't judge a book by its cover* _____

_____

_____

_____

_____

20. *Down to the wire* _____

_____

_____

_____

_____

21. *Going the extra mile* _____

_____

_____

_____

_____

22. *A piece of cake* _____

_____

_____

_____

_____

23. *Jump through hoops* _____

_____

_____

_____

_____

24. *To go out on a limb* _____

_____

_____

_____

Building Characterization

Directions: Select a character from a novel. In teams, discuss each question. After discussing each question, write your own answer.

1. What are the character's physical traits? _____

_____

_____

_____

2. How does the character you chose interact with the other characters? _____

_____

_____

_____

3. How do other characters view the character you selected? _____

_____

_____

4. What do you learn about the character's background through the other characters? _____

_____

_____

5. What dialogues provide clues to the character's beliefs? _____

_____

_____

_____

6. As the reader, what interpretations do you make about the character? _____

_____

_____

_____

"To Build a Fire"
Writing About a Novel

Directions: In teams, take turns sharing important skills needed to survive a disaster. Then, in turn, share the specific skills the man lacked to survive the disaster. Finally, independently write a one-page paper describing skills that would have helped the man survive.

Teammates Consult—"To Build a Fire"